SIMPLE
FOR T

The Sierra Club Outdoor Activities Guides

SIMPLE FOODS FOR THE PACK

CLAUDIA AXCELL, DIANA COOKE
& VIKKI KINMONT

Illustrated by Bob Kinmont

Sierra Club Books San Francisco

The Sierra Club, founded in 1892 by John Muir, has devoted itself to the study and protection of the earth's scenic and ecological resources—mountains, wetlands, woodlands, wild shores and rivers, deserts and plains. The publishing program of the Sierra Club offers books to the public as a nonprofit educational service in the hope that they may enlarge the public's understanding of the Club's basic concerns. The point of view expressed in each book, however, does not necessarily represent that of the Club. The Sierra Club has some sixty chapters coast to coast, in Canada, Hawaii, and Alaska. For information about how you may participate in its programs to preserve wilderness and the quality of life, please address inquiries to Sierra Club, 730 Polk Street, San Francisco, CA 94109.

Library of Congress Cataloging in Publication Data

Axcell, Claudia, 1946–
Simple foods for the pack.

Previous ed. by Vikki Kinmont and Claudia Axcell. 1976. Bibliography: p. Includes index.

1. Outdoor cookery. 2. Backpacking. 3. Cookery (Natural foods) I. Cooke, Diana. II. Kinmont, Vikki, 1944–. III. Sierra Club.   IV. Title. TX823.A92 1986   641.5'78
85–22076 ISBN 0–87156–757–1

Front cover photograph by Keith Gunnar

Book design by Jon Goodchild

Illustrations by Bob Kinmont

Printed in the United States of America

First revised edition

10 9 8 7 6 5 4 3

The man who sat on the ground in his tipi meditating on life and its meaning, accepting the kinship of all creatures and acknowledging unity with the universe of things was infusing into his being the true essence of civilization. And when native man left off this form of development, his humanization was retarded in growth.

—Chief Luther Standing Bear

ACKNOWLEDGMENTS

Together we thank Bob Kinmont for the illustrations, and Dr. Bob Denton and Dr. John Christopher for help on the natural remedies section.

Claudia thanks Michael Kaiserski, her husband, for his love and support and Diana for her expertise and for being a part of this revision.

Diana thanks Michael, her husband, for his constant support and encouragement.

CONTENTS

■■

I picked my way
Through a mountain road,
And I was greeted
By a smiling violet.

Bashō

INTRODUCTION

This book is a guide to using natural foods while backpacking. It shows you how to carry simple meals that offer nourishment, balance, low cost and good health. The foods are lightweight and long-lasting, and the recipes easily packed and prepared.

In the ten years since the original edition was first published natural foods have become an everyday item in most kitchens, and the recent emphasis on physical fitness has helped raise public consciousness on the importance of good food.

In this edition we've included more and different kinds of foods and more recipes. They're better tasting, too. We've got some exotic dishes like Hot and Sour Soup, Moroccan Couscous, and Salmon in Tomato Orange Sauce. Everywhere we've tried to find what is simply prepared and delicious, like our breads to make in camp, Chocolate Fudge Pudding and Spice Cake. You *can* prepare and pack delectable foods in the back country.

We've also updated medical information and added new material about the use of fires and the treatment of water.

We are happy to share these recipes with you and hope that they will be of help, and that you will enjoy expanding on them as you discover new possibilities.

CARING FOR THE BACKCOUNTRY

Carry and use a stove for all your cooking. Natural fuel wood fires are not allowed in many areas.

Carry out *all* garbage.

Camp at least 100 feet away from all water sources.

Do all washing at least 100 feet away from water sources. If you must use soap, use biodegradable soap, sparingly.

To make a sanitary latrine: walk at least 100 feet away from all water sources. Dig a hole several inches into the dirt. Deposit wastes including toilet paper (use white—many dyes are not biodegradable) and bury well. Tamp down.

WATER

Water is the one backcountry nutrient we cannot live without.

Backcounty water looks clean and inviting bubbling over rocks and cascading into remote valleys; however, a real threat of contracting giardiasis and other water-borne diseases now exists. Even the upper reaches of your favorite watershed may have been contaminated by the poor sanitation habits of wilderness users and local critters. (Giardiasis was known as "beaver-fever" at one time.)

Giardiasis, a worldwide problem, is caused by *Giardia lamblia,* a protozoan that is transmitted through the excrement of animals and humans. It occurs in two stages, trophozoite and cyst, the cyst being the more dangerous of the two stages. Symptoms appear 7 to 21 days after the cyst is ingested and may include chronic diarrhea, abdominal cramps, bloating, fatigue, and loss of weight. Treatment by prescription drugs is necessary to kill the organism.

Water weighs about 9 pounds a gallon, making it impractical to carry your daily water needs long distances. An ounce of prevention is the attitude to take when using water in the backcountry. There are three widely used methods available to protect yourself: boiling water, chemical treatment, and filtration.

BOILING WATER

Boil water hard for 2–3 minutes at sea level; add 1 minute for every 2,000 feet of altitude. Unfortunately, there are two disadvantages to boiling water: The water will taste flat (adding a pinch of salt, a vitamin C tablet, or a squeeze of lemon juice will help improve the flavor), and it takes a lot of time and fuel to boil enough water for your needs.

CHEMICAL TREATMENT

Many factors make this treatment unreliable. CHLORINE PURIFIERS have been found to be less than 100% effective against *Giardia*.

IODINE PURIFIERS are more effective. The three widely used acceptable iodine methods are:

Prepared Iodine Tablets (TGHP): Iodine tablet shelf names are Globaline, Coughlans, and Potable Aqua. They have been used for many years; however, effective destruction of *Giardia* cysts depends on accurate control of water temperature and contact duration.

Iodine Crystals: These are obtainable through a pharmacist. Add 4 to 8 grains of crystals to a 1-ounce vial of water, making a saturated solution. Add *this* solution, strained from the crystals, by the capful (2.5cc), to a quart of water, and let it stand for 30 minutes to 1 hour before drinking.

The amount of solution to use depends on the temperature of water per quart:

37°F	8–10 capfuls
68°F	5–6 capfuls
77°F	5 capfuls
104°F	4 capfuls

The crystals may be used many times.

Ingesting a crystal is extremely dangerous—iodine is toxic. Persons with thyroid problems should not use an iodine treatment at all.

Tincture of Iodine: This is another available iodine purifier. It is a 2% solution and is added at the rate of 10–20 drops per quart (depending on water temperature).

FILTRATION

By remembering that the *Giardia* trophozoite measures 12–15 microns and the cyst is 8–12 microns, you can determine the best type of filter to use:

Straw-Type Filters: These use a 10-micron filter and usually an iodine purifier as well. They are not considered effective because of the filter size and the water's brief contact with iodine.

Portable Pumps: There are two brands available at present for backcountry use. The efficient European Katadyn pump weighs about 23 ounces, can filter a quart a minute, but is expensive. The filter is made of porcelain and is reusable after cleaning. America's General Ecologys First Need pump is widely available and weighs a mere 12 ounces. The 0.4-micron filter effectively removes *Giardia* and many other water-borne disease bacteria. The flow is about 1 pint a minute, and the lifespan of the disposable filter cartridge is up to 800 pints. There are backwash instructions to prolong the life of the cartridge. Water will cease to pass through the filter, "telling" you to replace the cartridge. The only disadvantage to a filtration purifier is the cost, but the pleasure of being able to taste pure mountain water again is priceless.

Practicing proper sanitation habits in the backcountry, and educating children about these habits, is a responsibility we all must share to prevent the spread of existing pollutants and the introduction of new strains.

STAPLES

Bran flakes: outer coating of the whole wheat berry. Good laxative, high in iron.

Bulgar or pilaf or ala: all of these are the same thing—cracked wheat that has been parboiled and dried. Needs only to be soaked in water.

Carob powder or St. John's bread: the ground pod from the honey locust tree. High in potassium, calcium, and phosphorous.

Chia seeds: Native Americans used chia to sustain them on their long marches. Concentrated in protein and food energy, these little seeds may be added to almost anything.

Corn: flour, grits, meal, polenta: all are whole (containing the germ) corn ground to different consistencies. Each type has a different use (refer to recipe index). (Also see Polenta.)

Couscous: a grainlike pasta made from durum wheat.

Date sugar: ground dried dates. A good sweetener.

Dried fruits: apricots, peaches, pears, apples, dates, figs, raisins, currants, prunes. Unsulphured, quick, sweet energy.

Fish and seafood: clams, shrimp, tuna, bonita, anchovies, fish flakes, trout, iriki, salmon, crab.

Flaxseed: untreated, high in phosphorous and niacin. Its mucilaginous quality aids in digestion and has a laxative effect.

Fruit juice concentrates: liquid-concentrated juice from fruits and berries, found in natural food stores. Somewhat expensive, but a little bit adds a lot of fresh vitamins. A good thing to take along on winter trips.

Garam masala: a blend of aromatic spices such as

cardamom, cloves, and cinnamon. Each blend varies. Available in ethnic food stores.

Garlic, garlic granules, garlic powder: fresh garlic is lightweight, easy to carry, and a good body builder and cleanser. We carry lots of it and use it freely. If it's inconvenient to use fresh garlic, substitute ½ teaspoon garlic powder or ¼ teaspoon garlic granules per clove of garlic. Garlic powder is dried ground garlic, and garlic granules are dried and ground garlic juice.

Grains: unrefined whole grains, flours, and pastas—amaranth, barley, buckwheat, corn, millet, oats, quinoa, rice, rye, wheat. High in B vitamins and protein.

Herbs: whole dried parsley, dill, tarragon, sweet basil, thyme, oregano, chervil, rosemary, bay leaf, cumin, sage, savory.

Honey: natural, raw. Honey not only takes the place of sugar, but has added food value. It's easy to carry in a plastic bottle, and its weight comes out about the same as refined sugar because of its concentrated sweetness. Generally, substitute half as much for sugar.

Legumes: garbanzos, soybeans, mung beans, peanuts.

Lentils: the common Egyptian lentil is found in most supermarkets. Decorticated lentils are split and have had their outer husk removed, reducing the cooking time. These are available in ethnic food stores as Dal.

Milk powder, noninstant: whole, low-fat, or skim. Use to fortify most foods; adds protein and calcium. *Instant:* instant powdered milk may be used but has slightly lower food value.

Miso: a salty paste made from fermented soybeans, rice, or wheat; a highly concentrated protein.

Noodles: see Pasta.

Nuts and nut butters: almonds, pecans, pine nuts, cashews, brazils, filberts, and walnuts. Another highly concentrated food, rich in protein, calcium, and phosphorous. Use sparingly, a little every day. Almonds and pine nuts are the highest in protein.

Oils: vegetable, nut, and seed: unrefined, unhydrogenated. Some recipes call for a specific oil if we feel that it has its own taste and food value. However, you may substitute your favorite or a general mild-flavored one like safflower or corn oil.

Parmesan cheese: highest in protein of all cheeses. Also lightweight and easy to carry. For the best flavor, grate fresh. Wedges of fresh Parmesan can be found in most supermarkets.

Pasta: whole-grain and vegetable, available in natural food stores.

Polenta: dried corn that has been ground to an even consistency. Sold in Italian food stores.

Quinoa: a recently rediscovered grain from Peru. A complete protein. High in vitamins and minerals. The mother grain. (See recipe index.)

Rice: Basmati—a whole-grain white rice from Pakistan. Wild rice—instant. Brown rice—whole grain, short or long.

Rose hip powder: the fruit of the rose bush, dried and ground. High in vitamin C.

Seaweed: hijiki, nori, kombu, wakame. Lightweight and very nourishing. Don't take them along and then experiment with your taste. Try them before you go, as their unusual flavor is delightful to some and overwhelming at first to others.

Seeds: like nuts, seeds are concentrated protein, only easier to digest. High in vitamins and minerals. Use freely: pumpkin, sesame, sunflower, . . .

Sesame seeds: unhulled, raw. Higher in calcium

than milk. A good source of potassium and phosphorous. An excellent backpacking food as the body needs more of these minerals when exerting energy.

Sesame seed butter: ground, hulled sesame seeds. Available raw or roasted.

Sesame tahina: sesame butter ground from unhulled sesame seeds. Raw or roasted.

Soy grits: cracked soybeans. A good source of protein. Quick cooking.

Soy milk powder: milk powder made from soybeans.

Spices: whole or ground fresh—allspice, cardamom, cinnamon, cloves, coriander, curry powder, fennel, fenugreek, ginger, nutmeg. To keep spices fresh, store in freezer.

Tamari soy sauce: a salty, tasty condiment made from soybeans. Good on grains, noodles, patties, and in soups.

Tomato flakes: available from backpacking stores.

Tomato paste: in tubes; it's very strong and can be found in gourmet food stores.

Tomato powder: available from backpacking supply stores. Very concentrated, a little goes a long way.

Tomatoes—sundried: now available in most supermarkets in the produce section. Distributed by Frieda and dried in the U.S.A. Also dried Italian tomatoes, found in specialty food stores.

Vegetable bouillon cubes and powder: make a balanced potassium broth.

Vegetable flakes: vegetable flakes are available mixed or individually, such as celery, bell pepper, onion, and chives. Found in the spice section in supermarkets.

Wheat germ: the untreated embryo of the wheat berry. High in B vitamins.

TOOLS

This is a list of the tools we use for cooking on the trail. We feel we need everything on this list, and suggest it as a guideline; however, there are no two packs alike.

frying pan
cooking pots, large and small, with lids,
    stainless or enamel
bowl, medium-sized, one per person
cup, drinking, and/or measuring
pocketknife, spoon, chopsticks
pancake turner
wooden stir spoon
strainer, small
grater (optional), small
can opener, small
hot pad
plastic bottles and containers, assortment
plastic bags
pot scrubber
matches
safety pins
biodegradable soap
aluminum foil
rope or cord
camp stove and fuel
trivet
heat diffuser
mini-oven (optional)
string

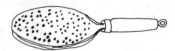

STOVES

Stoves are now considered a must for backcountry traveling. Firewood is scarce, and natural fuel wood fires are banned in many areas, and have a heavy impact on the delicate wilderness environment. Stoves have a minimal impact on the wilderness, and when traveling into snow country they are a necessity for melting snow for water.

There are three types of stoves available: butane, white gas, and kerosene.

Butane: Butane cartridge stoves are convenient and inexpensive to use. There is no liquid fuel to carry or spill. The stoves are easy to light, have an immediate maximum heat output, and the flame is as easy to control as turning a knob. Replacement cartridges are available in Europe as well as America, but disposal is a problem. Remember to keep your empty cartridges with you until they can be properly disposed of. Another problem with butane stoves is that the cartridges must be kept above freezing for effective operation. Also, a cartridge cannot be changed until it is empty, and as the fuel decreases, the heat output decreases.

White Gas: Some advantages to using a white gas stove are that white gas is highly volatile and evaporates readily when spilled. White gas burns hot so it is good for quick cooking or for melting large amounts of snow for water. The fuel can also be used for priming, so extra need not be carried. But the fuel is highly flammable and does consume oxygen rapidly. Be sure that your area as well as the stove is well ventilated. Self-pressurizing stoves must be insulated from snow or cold. Do not use automotive gas in a white gas stove. It will clog the burner and cause the stove to malfunction or possibly explode.

Kerosene: A worldwide fuel, kerosene is readily available almost anywhere. Spilled fuel won't easily ignite, and the stove can sit directly on the snow. Kerosene stoves have a high heat output, are less complicated, and have fewer mechanical difficulties than white gas stoves. Optional fuels such as diesel oil #1, Stoddards solvent, and home heating oil can be used successfully. Kerosene stoves need to be primed.

For further information concerning stoves, check with your local mountaineering supply store.

HINTS

Backpacking, canoeing, climbing—just playing outside puts a lot of stress on our bodies. We need more protein to replace muscle; liquids and salts to replace what we sweat away; fats to help us keep warm; B vitamins to keep nerves and muscles working; and quick-energy foods for fuel. Appetites get bigger, too, so we have allowed for large servings in the recipes. If you are going up high, drinking lots of water will help you to acclimatize faster.

Most of the ingredients used in the recipes may be in your cupboard at home, or they can be easily obtained from natural food and local grocery stores. A note on tuna: Dolphins swim with yellowfin tuna and are killed right along with them. So we suggest you buy albacore tuna or bonita.

A simple way to package the meals is to put all the dry ingredients for one recipe in a plastic bag (some recipes require two bags), label it, and add liquids in camp. We like to use the "zip-locking" type of plastic bags since they close airtight, taking up less volume in the pack and keeping the food fresher. Wide-mouth plastic bottles are good for liquids and condiments such as oil, soy sauce, peanut butter, and honey; and plastic tubes are suitable for packing liquids, butters, and pastes. To organize the food in your pack, put all the suppers in one stuff bag, breakfasts in another, and lunches in a third, leaving the condiments in a fourth bag by themselves. For another way of packaging your food, see the section entitled Grab Bag.

BASIC STEAMING DIRECTIONS

After charring many breads, cakes, and puddings over the fierce flame of a backpacking stove, we have developed this method of steaming. It takes from 10 to 30 minutes longer to steam, but is well worth the extra fuel and time. The foods turn out moist with little chance of burning.

You will need two pots, one nesting inside the other. The smaller should be approximately 7 inches in diameter with at least ¼ inch or more of space between it and the larger pot. Tight-fitting lids for both pots are ideal, but aluminum foil and string will also work. To make a lid, crimp foil tightly over the pot and tie it securely with string. Make sure the foil has no holes in it. If your pots are thin it is a good idea to carry a wire trivet to place between them.

Oil the smaller pot and pour in the batter. Cover with a lid or foil securely tied with string. Place into the larger pot, into which you add enough water to come half-way up the side of the smaller pot. Cover tightly. Keep the water at a steady boil.

Don't peek until the minimum cooking time is up. Use a pot mitt to prevent a steam burn.

PRESSURE COOKER IN THE BACKCOUNTRY?

Even though pressure cookers are heavier than regular camp pots, they are becoming increasingly popular to take into the backcountry.

The advantage of pressure cooking is the reduced time it takes to cook foods, saving precious fuel and making it possible to cook your brown rice, whole grain, and bean recipes.

Pressure cookers demand respect, and time should be taken to read the manufacturer's instructions. The rubber valves and gaskets should be replaced each season if you use the cooker frequently.

Overfilling is the main reason for pressure cooker malfunction. Foods that expand, such as rice and beans, should be no more than half-way up the cooker. Never fill the cooker more than two-thirds full.

Altitude does affect the cooking times according to the following chart:

increase time by

5% for up to 3,000 feet
10% for up to 4,000 feet
15% for up to 5,000 feet
20% for up to 6,000 feet
25% for up to 7,000 feet
30% for up to 8,000 feet

Once you have mastered your particular pressure cooker, there is no end to the recipes you can use.

1.

FOODS TO MAKE
AT HOME

The following foods are to be prepared at
home before you go. They are
concentrated, high-energy foods. A little
goes a long way. Add them to your usual
menu for extra nutrition and fresh
homemade flavors, or carry them in your
pack for trips when you aren't going to
cook and need strength-giving food.

JOURNEY CAKES

Small cakes, made at home, before the trip.
They are high in food value, easy to carry,
and long-lasting. Journey Cakes are good
for any meal or snack, adding a fresh taste.
They also help round out a meal of cheese
or nuts when cooking is impossible.

POLENTA CAKES

¶ 1 dozen

Because they contain fresh vegetables, these
Polenta Cakes are like small casseroles. They are
good accompaniments to soups or fried fish for
supper or with cheese for lunch. They always seem
to be the first to go out of your pack.

1 cup polenta *or* corn grits
2 tablespoons soy grits
1 teaspoon salt
4 cups water
2 onions, minced
2 carrots, grated
2 zucchini, grated
2 garlic cloves, minced
4 tablespoons sesame butter
½ cup sunflower seeds
3 tablespoons honey (optional)
1 tablespoon chia seeds (optional)
¼ cup milk powder (optional)

In a saucepan, bring the water and salt to a boil.
Stir in polenta and soy grits, bring back to a boil,
cover pan, and reduce heat to low. Cook for 15–20
minutes. The mixture should be very thick.
Remove from heat and set aside until cool and
firm. Meanwhile, sauté the vegetables and garlic
in 2 tablespoons of oil until they are browned and
dry. Remove from heat and stir in remaining ingredients. Cool. Combine the two mixtures well until
there are no lumps of polenta. Use your hands if
need be. Form into 12 patties approximately 3
inches in diameter and ½-inch thick. Place on a
slightly greased cookie sheet and bake in moderate
oven (350°) for 30 minutes, turning once.
The cakes will be brown and firm. Cool before
packaging.

Food Processor Method: With the machine running,

drop the garlic through the feed tube to mince. Add the onion and turn machine off to finely chop. Replace the blade with the shredding disc and shred the carrots and zucchini directly on top of the onion. Complete as in the preceding directions.

Variations: Use nut butters in place of sesame butter; use leftover vegetables (mash before adding); use nuts or pumpkin seeds in place of sunflower seeds; season with mixed herbs.

POTATO CAKES

Fresh potato flavor, moist and ready to eat out of your pack. Or, for a full meal serve with Miso Mustard Sauce or plain mustard or horseradish. Also good with Cream of Tomato Soup or Tomato Orange Sauce.

6 medium raw russet potatoes, with peels, grated
2 carrots, grated
2 onions, chopped
2 garlic cloves, minced
1 teaspoon mixed herbs (optional)
2 eggs, beaten
3 tablespoons melted butter
1 teaspoon salt
pinch cayenne
¼–½ cup whole wheat bread crumbs
½–1 cup Parmesan cheese (optional)

In a bowl, mix all ingredients thoroughly. Spread in an 8 by 12 inch pan. Bake at 350° for 1 hour. Cut into squares; cool. Wrap individually in wax paper.

Food Processor Method: With the machine running, drop the garlic through the feed tube to mince. Add the onions and turn the machine on and off several times to finely chop. Replace the blade with the shredding disc, and shred the potatoes directly on top of the onions, using moderate pressure on the plunger. Set aside in a bowl. Replace the blade and combine all the remaining ingredients and add them to the reserved potato mixture. Mix and bake as above.

CARROT CAKES

¶ 15 squares

Great as they are or as a vegetable with dinner. For sweet all-carrot flavor, omit the onion.

6 cups shredded carrots (about 10 medium carrots, 1½ pounds)
1 small onion, chopped
2 garlic cloves, crushed
¼ cup whole wheat flour
½ cup whole wheat bread crumbs
2 eggs, beaten
1 cup Parmesan cheese, fresh grated
grind of fresh pepper
pinch of nutmeg

Combine all the ingredients and mix well. Spread into a greased 13 by 18 inch pan and cover with foil. Bake for 45 minutes at 350°, remove the foil, and bake for a further 15 minutes.

Cool the pan on a rack, and cut the cakes into squares while warm. Remove them from the pan when cold and wrap individually in wax paper.

Food Processor Method: With metal blade in place and the machine running, drop the garlic through the feed tube to mince. Add the onion and turn on and off to finely chop. Add bread and pulse the machine to make crumbs. Add eggs, cheese, and seasonings, and turn on machine to combine. Replace the metal blade with the shredding disc and shred the carrots directly on top of the egg mixture. Stir ingredients to combine and then proceed as above.

WALNUT CHEESE BURGERS

These cakes are rich and hearty. Serve them with
Miso Mustard or Miso Horseradish Sauce, or with
soup for dinner. Good plain out of your pack, too.

2 cups cheddar cheese, grated
2 cups walnuts *or* pecans, ground
1 cup sesame seeds
½ cup sunflower seeds
½ cup raw wheat germ
½ cup fresh parsley, minced fine
4 scallions, minced fine
3 large eggs

Combine all ingredients, beating in eggs to mix
thoroughly. Form into patties and bake on a
cookie sheet in a moderate oven (350°) for 30
minutes, turning once, or sauté in a skillet. Cool
before packing in airtight zip-locking plastic bag
or a plastic container with a lid.

These cakes can also be made in camp and served
hot. Just mix all ingredients, except eggs, at home
in a zip-locking plastic bag. In camp, add the eggs,
mix well, form into patties, and sauté.

Food Processor Method: With metal blade in place
finely chop the parsley and scallions. Set aside.
With metal blade in place, chop the nuts by turning the machine on and off until the nuts are finely
chopped. Add the sesame and sunflower seeds,
wheat germ, and eggs—pulse the machine to combine. Add to the scallions and parsley. Place the
shredding disc on the machine and shred the
cheese. Add to the reserved mixture, mix, and
complete as above.

SOYBEAN BURGERS

A hearty rich flavor, good with cheese and mustard, or serve the burgers with Tomato Sauce or Mushroom Sauce.

1 cup dry soybeans, soaked overnight and cooked
    approximately 2 hours
1 onion, chopped fine
4 garlic cloves, minced
1 tablespoon fresh parsley, minced
1 tablespoon oil
1 tablespoon miso
1 teaspoon tamari soy sauce

Mash the beans well. Add the remaining ingredients and mix well. The mash should be very thick and hold well when shaped into a ball. Form into patties 3 inches in diameter and bake on a cookie sheet in a moderate oven(350°) for about 30 minutes. Turn once while baking. Cakes are done when they feel solid. They will be crusty on the outside and soft inside. Cool before packaging in airtight zip-locking plastic bags or a plastic container with lid.

Food Processor Method: With the metal blade in place and the machine running, drop the garlic through the feed tube to mince. Add the parsley and turn the machine on and off several times to finely chop the parsley. Add the cooked soybeans, turn the machine on and off, and then let the machine run to mash the beans. Add the remaining ingredients through the feed tube while the machine is running. Do not overprocess the beans to a paste. Then proceed as above.

Variations: Add a grated carrot; season with 1 teaspoon cumin and ½ teaspoon chili powder; season with oregano; serve with mustard.

FALAFEL

¶ 1 dozen

A spicy Middle Eastern snack. Serve in pocket bread with Tahini Dipping Sauce, or eat it out of your pack as a snack along the trail.

2 cups garbanzo beans
½ cup each celery and scallions, chopped
3 garlic cloves
2 teaspoons cumin seeds, crushed
1 teaspoon coriander seeds, crushed
½ teaspoon tumeric, ground
¼ teaspoon cayenne
2 eggs
3 tablespoons sesame tahini
1 tablespoon lemon juice

Soak the beans for a few hours and then cook them in lots of water until tender, about 2 hours. Drain. Blend the beans in a blender or food processor until smooth. Or mash them well with a fork. Combine with the remaining ingredients and blend until evenly mixed. Chill for at least an hour.

With floured hands, shape into small balls the size of a walnut. Dust each ball with flour or fine bread crumbs.

Deep fry at 365° until golden brown; or shape into patties and sauté. Cool.

Carry the Falafel in a lidded plastic container.

To serve, stuff into pocket bread with slices of cucumber and Tahini Dipping Sauce.

LENTIL RICE CAKES

¶ 1 dozen

A complete protein. Good alone, or serve with Humus or Tahini Dipping Sauce.

⅔ cup brown rice
⅓ cup lentils
1 teaspoon salt
3 cups water
1 small onion, chopped fine
1 small carrot, grated
2 garlic cloves, minced
1 tablespoon fresh parsley, minced
1 tablespoon olive oil
1 teaspoon tamari soy sauce

Season with *one* of the following:

2–4 teaspoons cumin
2–4 teaspoons curry powder

In a saucepan, bring the rice, lentils, salt, and water to a boil, cover the pot, and reduce the heat to low. Cook 50–60 minutes. The mixture should be dry and all water absorbed. Allow to cool. Mash well with your hands, then add the rest of the ingredients, and mix well. Form into 3-inch patties, place on a greased cookie sheet, and bake at 350° for 30–45 minutes. Turn once to allow the underside to cook. Cool before packaging.

Food Processor Method: Chop the onion, carrot, parsley, and garlic finely with metal blade; add the remaining seasonings. Add the dry rice and lentil mixture and pulse several times to combine, but don't overprocess to a paste. Then proceed as above.

BROWN RICE CAKES

¶ 1 dozen

These are good for lunch with cheddar cheese or Port Salut. Or as an accompaniment to Cream of Tomato Soup or fish. Sprinkle soy sauce or spread mustard on top if desired.

1 cup brown rice
1 teaspoon salt
3 cups water
1 carrot, grated
1 onion, chopped fine
½ to 1 cup greens, chopped (spinach, mustard
    greens, or watercress)
1 tablespoon olive oil
2 teaspoons ground ginger

In a saucepan, bring rice, water, and salt to a boil. Cover the pot, reduce heat, and cook 60 minutes. Allow to cool. Mash well with your hands, add the rest of the ingredients, and continue to mix and mash with your hands. If too moist, add a little soy flour. Form into 3 by ½ inch patties, and bake on a greased cookie sheet for 30 minutes at 350°, turning once. Cool before packaging.

Food Processor Method: Mash the cooked rice and flavorings in the processor by turning the machine on and off several times, scraping down the bowl occasionally. Do not overprocess to a paste. Then proceed as above.

ORIENTAL BROWN RICE CAKES

‖‖‖‖‖‖‖‖‖‖‖‖‖‖‖‖‖‖‖‖‖‖‖‖‖‖‖‖‖‖‖‖‖‖

¶ 1 dozen

A good accompaniment to Hot and Sour Soup or good dipped in Sweet and Sour Sauce.

1 cup brown rice
1 teaspoon salt
2½ cups water
1 carrot, grated
2 cloves garlic, minced
1 tablespoon toasted sesame oil
1 teaspoon fresh ginger root, grated
2 tablespoons fermented black beans, chopped
    (optional)

In a saucepan, bring water, salt, and rice to a boil. Cover the pan and reduce the heat to low. Cook for 40–60 minutes. Cool. Add the remaining ingredients and mash well with your hands. Form into 3 by ½ inch patties and bake on an oiled cookie sheet for 30–45 minutes in a 350° oven, turning once. Cool on a rack before packaging.

Food Processor Method: Mash the cooked rice and flavorings in the processor by turning the machine on and off several times, scraping down the bowl occasionally. Do not overprocess to a paste. Then proceed as above.

MILLET SEED CAKES

Serve these cakes for dinner with Cream of Tomato Soup or a mild broth. They are a spicy treat with Humus or a nut butter.

1 cup millet
2 garlic cloves, crushed
1 carrot, finely chopped
2½ cups water
6 cardamom pods
¼ cup sesame seeds
1 teaspoon coriander
1 teaspoon cinnamon
½ teaspoon fennel seeds
¼ cup fenugreek
salt and pepper to taste

Cook the millet, garlic, and carrot in 2½ cups of water in a saucepan with the lid on, for 20 minutes. Meanwhile grind the seeds and spices together with mortar and pestle, coffee grinder, or electric mill till finely mashed. When the millet has cooked, stir in the seeds, spices, salt, and pepper, and mash well with a fork. It will mash to a paste. Allow to cool enough so you can handle it. Shape into 3 by ½ inch thick cakes. Place on an oiled cookie sheet and bake at 350° for 30 minutes, turning once. Cool on a rack before packaging.

MILLET DATE ORANGE CAKES

These sweet orange-scented cakes are a tasty quick snack.

1 cup millet
1 cup dates, pitted and chopped
rind of 1 orange
1 cup walnuts, finely chopped
2–3 tablespoons honey
2 tablespoons oil

Cook the millet in 2½ cups of water in a saucepan with the lid on, for 20 minutes. Mash with a fork to a paste. When cool enough to handle, add the dates, orange rind, walnuts, honey, and oil. Mix well with your hands or blend in a food processor to combine.

Shape into 3 by ½ inch thick cakes and place them on an oiled cookie sheet. Bake at 350° for 30 minutes or until brown on both sides. Turn once. Cool the cakes on a wire rack before packaging.

PUMPKIN PIE CAKES

¶ 1 dozen

These are a real treat for dessert. Spread them with cream cheese or eat them plain.

1 to 1½ cups cooked pumpkin *or* yams
½ cup water
½ cup rolled oats
½ cup cornmeal
¼ cup maple syrup or honey
2 teaspoons cinnamon
1 teaspoon ginger
¼ teaspoon nutmeg
pinch cloves *or* 1 tablespoon pumpkin pie spice
1 egg

Soak the rolled oats in ½ cup boiling water until the water is absorbed, and then combine the oats with the remaining ingredients. Mix well. Drop, from a spoon, onto an oiled cookie sheet, and smooth out the tops with the back of the spoon. The cakes should be about 3 inches in diameter by ½ inch thick. Bake in a moderate oven (350°) for 40 minutes, turning once. Cool. Wrap individually in waxed paper.

COCONUT ALMOND BARLEY CAKES

A sweet Journey Cake that is wonderful spread with nut butter or just eaten plain.

¼ cup barley
3 cups water
½ cup blanched toasted almonds, chopped fine
    (toast in 350° oven for 8 minutes)
¼ cup unsweetened shredded or macaroon
    coconut
1 tablespoon honey
grating of fresh nutmeg

Cook the barley in the water, with the lid on the saucepan, until very tender, about 1 hour. Add more water if the barley absorbs the water before becoming tender. Cool. Mash with the remaining ingredients using your hands to combine well. Shape into 3 by ½ inch patties and bake on an oiled cookie sheet at about 350° for 20–30 minutes, or until firm and brown; turn once. Cool on a rack. Wrap when cold in wax paper or plastic wrap.

Food Processor Method: Cook the barley as above. Then pulse all the ingredients and the cooked barley with the metal blade to combine, scraping down the bowl. Do not overprocess to paste. Proceed as above.

SEED CAKES

This is a different-tasting cake, good with peanut butter and honey, cheese, hot mustard, any sauce or gravy, or just plain.

½ cup polenta *or* corn grits
2 tablespoons soy grits
2 cups water
½ teaspoon salt
1 cup sunflower seeds
½ cup pumpkin seeds
2 tablespoons sesame seeds
2 tablespoons chia seeds (optional)
1 teaspoon honey (optional)

In a saucepan bring the water and salt to a boil. Stir in the polenta and soy grits and bring back to a boil. Cover the pan, reduce the heat to low, and cook until very thick, 15–20 minutes. Allow to cool. Meanwhile, grind all the seeds except the chia seeds and a few sunflower seeds. When the polenta mixture is cool, add the seeds, salt, and honey. Mix well with your hands, and form into patties approximately 3 inches in diameter. Bake on a greased cookie sheet in a moderate oven (350°) for 30 minutes, turning once. Cool before packaging.

Food Processor Method: Follow the preceding directions but combine the cooked polenta and remaining ingredients in the processor, with the metal blade, turning the machine on and off until the mixture is uniform.

BREADS
& CRACKERS

There are so many wonderful bread recipes
available that we didn't feel it necessary to
include very many. But here are a few we
thought were special. They are high in
protein, one is made with leftovers, and all
can be used to accompany any meal or be
eaten at any time.

For additional bread recipes, see "Breads to
Make in Camp"

ZWIEBACK

This is a good idea for any whole-grain yeasted bread. It makes the bread lightweight and long-lasting. Zwieback may be broken into soups or salads to add crunchiness.

Slice bread ½ inch thick or a little thicker and bake on open oven racks at 225° for approximately 2½ hours. Carry in a plastic bag.

HIGH-PROTEIN CRACKERS

¶ 2 dozen

Serve these for lunch or supper. They take the place of bread and are tasty and crunchy.

1 cup whole wheat flour
1 cup rye flour
½ cup soy flour
½ cup raw wheat germ
½ cup sesame seeds
1 tablespoon chia seeds (optional)
1 teaspoon coarse-ground sea salt
⅓ cup oil
enough cold water to make a stiff dough

In a bowl, combine dry ingredients, except salt, and mix well. Stir in the oil and mix to an even consistency. Add water to make a stiff dough. Knead 10–20 times and let stand a few minutes. On a floured surface, roll the dough very thin, sprinkle on salt and a few extra sesame seeds, and roll again, pushing the salt and seeds well into the dough. Make holes with a fork, and then cut into desired shapes. Bake on an ungreased cookie sheet at 300° until golden brown and crisp, about 15–20 minutes. Cool before packaging.

SESAME CHIA CRACKERS

¶ approximately 2 dozen

Crunchy crackers that are easy to make.

2 cups whole wheat flour *or* 1½ cups oat flour and
     ¾ cup soy flour
½ cup sesame seeds
2 tablespoons chia seeds
1 teaspoon salt
⅓ cup sesame oil
½ cup water

In a bowl, mix flour, sesame and chia seeds, and
salt. Stir in the oil and mix to an even consistency.
Add the water and shape into a large ball. Sprinkle
extra sesame seeds on wax paper and roll the
dough about ¼ inch thick. Cut into cracker
shapes. Remove the crackers from wax paper,
place on an ungreased cookie sheet, and bake at
375° for 15–20 minutes. Cool before packaging.

CORN CRACKERS

¶ 2 dozen

2 cups whole wheat flour
1 cup cornmeal
½ cup sesame seeds
pinch salt
¼ cup oil
2 tablespoons honey
1 cup water, approximately

Combine all the dry ingredients. Mix together the oil, honey, and water and add to the dry ingredients. Mix well with your hands, adding extra water if necessary. On a floured surface roll the dough about ¼ inch thick. Bake on an oiled cookie sheet at about 350° for 20 minutes or until crisp and lightly browned. Cool before packaging.

GRAHAM CRACKERS

¶ 3 dozen

These are far removed from store-bought ones; they're less fragile and very filling.

¾ cup butter
½ cup honey
1 teaspoon vanilla
3 cups graham *or* whole wheat flour
½ cup raw wheat germ
1 teaspoon cinnamon
½ teaspoon baking powder
¾ cup water

Beat together the butter, honey, and vanilla until fluffy. Combine the dry ingredients and add alternately with the water to the creamed mixture. Roll out on a floured surface to about ¼ inch thick, cut into squares, and place on an ungreased cookie sheet. Prick each cookie a couple of times. Bake for 20–25 minutes at 325° or until nicely browned. Cool on a rack before packaging.

SESAME SEED BREAD

A little of this bread goes a long way, so slice it thin. The sweet, nutty flavor of sesame comes out very well when the bread is toasted. It's a good accompaniment to soups.

1½ cups sesame seeds
1½ cups raw wheat germ
4 cups whole wheat flour
1 cup brown rice flour
1 cup millet flour
1½ teaspoons salt
1 tablespoon oil
3 cups water

Toast the sesame seeds and wheat germ separately in an ungreased frying pan, and then put in one bowl. Add the flours and salt and stir well. Make a well in the center and add the oil and water. Stir well. Spoon into a well-greased bread pan. Bake at 325° for 1¼ hours or until the bread is golden brown and feels firm. Remove from the pan and cool. For a soft crust, brush the top with a little oil while the bread is still hot.

HIGH-PROTEIN LEFTOVERS BREAD

¶ 2 loaves

This is a heavy, tasty bread that keeps well and,
when sliced thin, is excellent with soups
or spreads.

5 cups whole wheat flour *or* 4 cups whole wheat
    and 1 cup rye flour
1 cup soy flour
4 cups leftover cooked vegetables and grains,
    mashed or strained, *or*, if you have no
    leftovers, 3 cups cooked millet and 1 cup
    cooked carrots or other vegetables on hand,
    mashed or strained
¼ cup of oil
2 teaspoons salt
vegetable stock or water, as needed
cornmeal for dusting pans

Mix all the ingredients completely, adding a little
whole wheat flour if the mixture is too sticky or a
little vegetable stock if it is too dry. Knead the
dough until it has a very even consistency and is
springy. Divide in half and shape into loaves. Put
into two oiled pans that have been sprinkled with
coarse cornmeal, and make a slit about ¼ inch
deep in the top of each loaf. Moisten the top with
water, cover the pans, and let the dough sit in a
warm spot 6–12 hours. Bake at 350° for 1 hour.
Remove from the pans and allow to cool before
packaging.

DRIED-FRUIT BREAD

¶ 3 small loaves

This is a heavy, sweet bread, high in protein. It's good for snacks with peanut butter and Dried Fruit Jam or toasted for breakfast with honey.

3 cups rolled oats
1 cup dried apricots, chopped or cut with scissors
3 cups warm water
1 cup raisins
1 cup dates, pitted and chopped
1 cup mixed nuts, chopped
¼ cup honey
¼ cup oil
1 teaspoon anise seeds (optional)
¼ teaspoon salt
4–4¼ cups whole wheat flour
1 cup millet flour, toasted
½ cup rye flour
½ cup soy flour
¼ cup milk powder

In a large bowl, soak the oatmeal and apricots in the water for 15 minutes. In a frying pan over moderate heat, toast the millet flour, stirring constantly until the aroma changes (approximately 3–5 minutes). Cool. Add the raisins, dates, nuts, honey, oil, anise, and salt. Stir well. Mix the flours together. Slowly add them and the milk powder to the other ingredients, and mix well with your hands. Turn out on a floured board and knead about 150 times. Form into three small loaves, place on a flat cookie sheet, and let sit for 6–12 hours. Slit the tops of the loaves, brush them lightly with oil, and bake at 350° for 1½ hours. Cool well before packaging.

BOSTON BROWN BREAD

¶ 2 1-lb. loaves

Smother this bread with cream cheese or nut butters for a delicious and filling lunch.

1 cup whole wheat flour
1 cup rye flour
1 cup cornmeal
2 teaspoons baking powder
1 teaspoon salt
2 cups buttermilk
1 cup raisins
⅔ cup molasses

Prepare two 1-pound coffee cans, or similar-size cans, by greasing and flouring to coat the insides well. Set aside.

Combine the dry ingredients. Stir together the buttermilk and the molasses, and add them with the raisins to the flour mixture. Stir well to combine.

Turn the mixture into the prepared coffee cans and cover each tightly with foil. Tie the foil securely with string. Place the cans on a rack or trivet in a saucepan with a tight-fitting lid. Pour boiling water in, to come at least half-way up the sides.

Boil for 3 hours, adding boiling water to maintain the level. Remove the can bottoms while the bread is still warm, and then cool the cans on a rack. When the cans are cool, push out the bread and slice it into ½-inch slices. Pack the slices back into the can and place plastic lids on each end. This makes a crush-proof container while hiking, and the container is easily flattened to pack out.

FRUITCAKE

¶ 2 loaves

Excellent luxury snack for winter escapades. Slice thin, wrap individually. It goes a long way.

1 pound butter
2 cups honey
1 tablespoon cinnamon
1 tablespoon cloves
1 tablespoon nutmeg
1 tablespoon allspice
2 teaspoons mace
1 teaspoon ginger
1 teaspoon salt
4½ cups whole wheat flour
½ cup brandy *or* apple, orange, prune, or
    grape juice
2 pounds currants
2 pounds dates
1½ pounds nuts
½ pound raisins

Cream the butter and honey together. Add the spices and salt and stir well. Add the flour alternately with ¼ cup of brandy or fruit juice. Fold in the dried fruits and nuts. Line the bottoms of two oiled loaf pans with parchment or brown paper cut into the right shapes. Oil again and pour in the cake batter. Place a shallow pan of water on the bottom shelf of the oven. Place the loaf pans on the upper shelf, and bake at 250° for 3–3½ hours or until done. Remove from the pans and cool.

Wrap the loaves in a cheesecloth that has been dipped in brandy or juice, pour ¼ cup brandy or juice over the top, and wrap airtight in foil. You may make this months before you eat it or only a week ahead of time. You can add ¼ cup brandy or fruit juice every couple of weeks or so. Just carefully open the foil, pour the liquid over the top, and reseal.

BOILED-FRUIT CAKE

¶ 1 8"-cake or 2 dozen fruit muffins

An Australian favorite. It's boiled to plump up the fruit, and then baked to finish.

4 cups dried fruits—raisins, golden raisins,
     currents, chopped apricots, peaches, prunes
1 cup water
¾ cup honey
1 cup butter
1 teaspoon baking soda
2 teaspoons cinnamon
½ teaspoon nutmeg
¼ teaspoon cloves
1 egg
1 cup whole wheat flour
1 cup unbleached flour
2 teaspoons baking powder

Place the first eight ingredients together in a saucepan and bring to a simmer with the lid on. Simmer 5 minutes. Allow to cool. Beat the egg. Sift together the flours and the baking powder. Stir the egg and flour into the fruit mixture. Mix to combine.

Turn into an 8-inch square pan that has been lined with butter or wax paper. Bake in a preheated 325°–350° oven for 1½ hours or until a cake tester comes out clean.

To bake as muffins, which are easier to pack and travel well, place in muffin papers in a muffin tin and bake for 25 minutes at 325°–359°.

POCKET FOODS

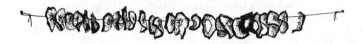

These are the foods that we like to keep within easy reach, for nourishment at any time. On the trail, for lunch, on a ski tour, in the tent at night or in the rain, floating down the river, sitting on a ledge or up in a tree. They provide condensed protein energy. And don't forget, just plain dried fruit and nuts make good Pocket Foods.

HOME-DRIED APPLES

Gravensteins, pippins, or delicious make the best dried apples, but any kind will do.

Wash the apples well. If they have been waxed, use castile soap. Remove the core and slice the apples in rings 1/8–1/4 inch thick. Hang the slices to dry on a string that goes through the center of each of the slices. Don't have the slices touch. Hang them for several days.

TRAIL CRUMBS

Mixtures of dried fruits, nuts, and seeds for munching any time. These are our favorite combinations, but don't feel limited.

almonds, Brazils, raisins, soy nuts, dates, carob chips

sunflower seeds and raisins

cashews, raisins, raw peanuts, sunflower seeds, rose hips

almonds and apricots

salted soy nuts and raisins

walnuts, dates, coconut chunks, sunflower seeds, carob chips

pecans and currants

pumpkin seeds and figs

pine nuts

FRUIT LEATHER

This is a dried fruit sweet treat. Break off pieces to suck on along the trail—it melts in your mouth, a good replacement for hard candy. When you have an excess of fresh ripe fruit or berries, plan ahead and dry some in thin shallow "peels" in the sun. It happens quickly and easily.

apricots
peaches
plums
all berries
apple or pear sauce that has
   been put through a ricer

Wash and dry the ripe fruit. Place the whole fruit in a ricer, and mash through into a bowl, leaving just the dry peels or seeds in the ricer. You might like to add almond extract, honey, or lemon juice, depending on taste.

Pour the fruit sauce in a puddle in the middle of a glass cake or pie pan and spread to within ½ inch of all edges. It should be the consistency of apple butter.

Place in the sun for the day, bringing it in as the sun goes down in order to avoid dew. Cover for the evening with an open paper bag or cheese-cloth to keep the fruit clean. Return to the sun the following day and repeat until dry. If a storm comes up for the day, put the pan in oven at the lowest heat possible and leave the door slightly open. Watch carefully. When the fruit is dry enough to be lifted off the pan, continue drying it on oven racks so both sides dry. In summertime, it should take 3 to 4 days. When finished, peel the leather off, lay it on a piece of wax paper or plastic wrap, and roll it up. Place the leather in a plastic bag and store it in a cool, dry, dark place.

TOASTED SOYBEANS

¶ approximately 1¼ cups

A crunchy snack, high in protein.

1 cup soybeans
4 cups water
soy sauce

Soak the soybeans in the water for 8–12 hours.
Strain and reserve the liquid for breads, soups,
and so forth. Place the drained beans in a shallow
baking pan and bake, stirring frequently, at 300°
for 75 to 90 minutes or until golden in color and
crunchy. When done, and still hot, sprinkle soy
sauce over the beans and stir until the sauce coats
them and dries up. Cool and then store in an airtight container.

Variations: Soak in salted water (1 teaspoon salt to
1 quart water) and omit the soy sauce. Also,
coarsely grind some of the beans and use them as
a condiment for soups, stews, salads, and so on.

SPICY SEED SNACK

These quantities may be varied according to taste.

1 cup pumpkin seeds
1 cup sunflower seeds
2 tablespoons toasted sesame oil
1 tablespoon tamari soy sauce
1 teaspoon curry powder
½ teaspoon cayenne
⅛ teaspoon garlic granules (optional)

Combine all the ingredients thoroughly. Sprinkle into a shallow baking pan. Bake in a 350° oven for 20–25 minutes, stirring occasionally. Store in an airtight container when cool.

Variation: Add assorted nuts to taste.

FRUIT PEMMICAN

Chewy fruit-nut bars, high in protein and good for eating on the trail or in your tent when it's pocket-food weather.

1 cup raisins
½ cup honey
½ cup milk powder
½ cup raw wheat germ
⅓ cup soy flour
¼ cup wheat bran
½ cup each almonds, walnuts, Brazils or filberts, whole or chopped
2 tablespoons oil
enough grape or apple juice to make a thick batter

Mix all ingredients well. Spread into a greased 8-inch square pan. Bake in 300° oven for 30–40 minutes or until firm. Cut into squares but allow to cool before removing from pan. Wrap individually.

Variation: Add dates or chopped apricots.

TRULY FRUITY BARS

¶ 19 × 13″ pan's worth

Yum!

FILLING
1 ½ cups dates, pitted
1 ½ cups raisins
½ orange, peeled
1 tablespoon grated lemon peel

CRUST
4 cups rolled oats
1 cup unsweetened coconut
½ cup soy flour
½ cup whole wheat pastry flour
½ cup honey
½ cup oil
1 teaspoon vanilla
½ teaspoon salt
pinch nutmeg
2 tablespoons dry malt (optional)

Put the filling ingredients through a coarse food grinder. Add more orange juice if needed. Mix the crumb crust ingredients and pat half the mixture into an oblong 9 by 13 inch cake pan. Spread the fruit mixture over this, and then pat the other half of crumb crust mixture on top. Be sure to cover all the fruit.

Bake at 350° for 30–40 minutes until golden brown. Cool slightly before cutting into bars. Cool completely before wrapping.

Variations: Substitute other dried fruits such as apricots and figs; figs and walnuts; peaches and dates; or raisins, currants, and apples.

GRANOLA

¶ approximately 1 gallon

Serve this granola with stewed fruit, hot or cold milk, water, mint or rose hip tea, or just plain dry as a pocket food.

½ cup oil
½ cup honey
½ cup sorghum, molasses, *or* maple syrup
1 tablespoon vanilla
¼ cup milk powder
2 tablespoons nutritional yeast
1 tablespoon orange *or* lemon peel, grated
1 cup raw wheat germ
5 cups rolled oats
2 cups rolled wheat
2 cups rolled rye
1 cup unsweetened coconut
2 cups raisins *or* currants
1 cup each cashews, almonds, pitted dates,
     sunflower seeds

Heat oil, honey, and syrup in a large pot until thin. Remove from heat. Add the remaining ingredients in the order given, except the fruit, nuts, and seeds. Stir well after each addition. Spread the mixture into two large ungreased cookie sheets with sides. Bake at 250° for 1½–2 hours, stirring occasionally. Cool. Stir in the remaining ingredients. Store in an airtight container.

For the trail, package in individual meal-size portions.

GRANOLA BARS

¶ 2 8″-square pans' worth

These are chewy, sweet, filling, satisfying, easy to pack, and good when your energy is low.

Follow the Granola recipe, using 6 cups of the rolled grains instead of 9. Press into two 8-inch square pans and bake at 300° for 30–40 minutes or until golden brown. Cut while hot, but cool before removing from pan.

RAW GRANOLA

¶ approximately 4 cups

Serve as is with milk, fruit juice, or hot tea. Or for a hot cereal, mix in boiling water.

1 cup rolled oats, chopped fine
1 cup rolled wheat, chopped fine
½ cup almonds, chopped small
½ cup filberts, chopped small
½ cup raw wheat germ
½ cup unsweetened coconut
½ cup dried apples, chopped small
½ cup raisins
2 tablespoons bran flakes
2 tablespoons dry grated lemon peel
1 tablespoon rose hip powder (optional)

Combine all the ingredients. Store in a covered jar. For the trail and convenience, package in meal-size portions.

CHEESE COOKIES

¶ approximately 2 dozen

½ pound medium cheddar cheese, grated
1 cup whole wheat flour
3 tablespoons oil
¼ teaspoon salt
dash cayenne
⅓ cup finely chopped pecans or walnuts, *or* save
    whole to put on top
3–4 tablespoons milk

Mix the grated cheese, flour, oil, salt, and cayenne
until they are an even crumbly texture. Add the
milk and chopped nuts and knead into a large
ball. Form balls about an inch in diameter and
mash them between your palms. If you didn't add
nuts to the mixture, place one-half nut meat into
the center top of each cookie. Bake in a 350° oven
on an oiled cookie sheet for 20 minutes.

ANZACS

¶ about 2 dozen

This is an original Australian recipe from World War I, when Australian women baked these biscuits (cookies) to send to their men on the beaches of Gallipoli. They were still fresh after an 8-week boat trip! Anzac stands for Australian–New Zealand Army Corps.

1 cup whole wheat flour
1 cup unsweetened coconut
1 cup brown sugar
1 cup rolled oats
½ cup butter
2 tablespoons water
½ teaspoon baking soda
1 tablespoon golden syrup, molasses, *or* honey

Combine the flour, coconut, sugar, and oats in a large bowl. Mix well. In a small saucepan melt the butter with the water, soda, and syrup. Add this to the dry ingredients, and mix well with your hands. Shape into cookies and bake on an oiled cookie sheet at 350° for about 20 minutes or until nice and brown. Cool on a rack.

HIGH-PROTEIN ALMOND COOKIES

¶ approximately 3 dozen

2¼ cups whole wheat flour
1 cup almond meal
¾ cup oat flour
½ cup chopped pecans
¼ cup soy flour
¼–½ cup currants *or* raisins
2 tablespoons chia seeds
1 teaspoon coriander
½ teaspoon salt
½ cup apple juice *or* water
½ cup honey
¼ cup oil
1 teaspoon almond extract

Mix all the dry ingredients in one bowl and the liquid ingredients in another. Combine the two and blend well. Form into 1-inch balls, place on an ungreased cookie sheet, and press down with a fork. Bake in a 350° oven for 15–20 minutes.

SESAME SEED COOKIES

¶ approximately 2 dozen

Crunchy, satisfying, high in protein.

1 cup sesame seeds
½ cup unsweetened coconut, grated or shredded
2 eggs
½ cup oil *or* butter
½ cup honey
1 teaspoon vanilla
2¼ cups whole wheat flour
½ teaspoon salt

In a skillet, over moderate heat, toast the seasame seeds and coconut until they are light brown; stir frequently. Combine the eggs, oil, honey, and vanilla, and then stir in the toasted seeds and coconut. Blend in the flour and salt, and stir well. Form into balls about an inch in diameter, place on an ungreased cookie sheet, and press with a fork. Bake at 325° for 15 minutes.

PEANUT BUTTER FUDGE

¶ approximately 1 pound

1 cup crunchy peanut butter
½ cup soy milk powder *or* regular milk powder
½ cup raisins
¼ cup sesame seeds
⅛ cup raw wheat germ
⅛–½ cup honey

Mix all ingredients together until they are
thoroughly blended. Carry in a lidded plastic
container and break off pieces as you wish.

CASHEW FUDGE

¶ approximately ¾ pound

½ cup cashew butter
½ cup chopped cashews
¼ cup currants *or* chopped raisins
¼ cup soy milk powder *or* ½ cup wheat germ
    flakes
2 tablespoons honey

Combine all the ingredients. Carry in a lidded
plastic container.

PECAN FUDGE

¶ approximately 1¾ pounds

½ cup honey
½ cup peanut butter
½ cup rolled oats (may be chopped or blended
    in blender)
½ cup unsweetened coconut
½ cup chopped pecans
2 tablespoons soy flour
1 tablespoon raw wheat germ
handful peanuts, sunflower seeds, and sesame
    seeds (may be chopped or ground)
2 teaspoons vanilla
1 teaspoon lemon juice

Mix in order: honey, peanut butter, oats, coconut,
pecans, soy flour, wheat germ, nuts and seeds,
vanilla, and lemon juice. Knead a little. Carry in a
lidded plastic container.

SESAME ALMOND FUDGE

¶ approximately 1 pound

1 cup sesame seeds
½ cup almonds
½ cup cashew butter *or* peanut butter
¼ cup currants *or* chopped raisins
2 tablespoons honey
1 tablespoon or more water

Grind the sesame seeds and almonds. Add the rest
of the ingredients, mix well, and pack in a lidded
plastic container.

SESAME BUTTER FUDGE

¶ approximately 1 pound

1 cup sesame butter
½ cup almonds, ground fine
¼ cup honey
handful of currants *or* raisins

Combine all the ingredients; knead well. Carry in a lidded plastic container.

CAROB FUDGE

¶ approximately ½ pound

1 cup sesame *or* sunflower seeds
2 tablespoons carob powder
2 tablespoons honey (optional)
1 tablespoon water

Grind the seeds, and mix all the ingredients well in a bowl. Pack in a lidded plastic container.

Variation: Add ¼ cup coconut; add ½ cup currants or chopped raisins.

SEED DATE FUDGE

¶ approximately 1¼ pounds

½ cup sesame seeds
½ cup sunflower seeds
1 tablespoon flax seeds
1 cup chopped dates
½ cup sesame butter
2 tablespoons chia seeds
¼ cup maple syrup (optional)

Grind sesame, sunflower, and flax seeds. Combine
them with the remaining ingredients, and mix
well with your hands. Carry in a lidded plastic
container.

DATE FIG FUDGE

¶ approximately ½ pound

1 cup dates, pitted
8 dried figs
½ cup walnuts *or* pecans

Put the ingredients through a food grinder, and
pack in a lidded plastic container.

APRICOT DATE FUDGE

¶ approximately 1½ pounds

1 cup apricots
1 cup dates
1 cup walnuts *or* pecans
handful of raisins *or* currants
2 tablespoons raw wheat germ
1 cup coconut, unsweetened macaroon
juice from ½ lime *or* lemon

Grind the fruit, nuts, and wheat germ in a
food grinder. Knead in the coconut and lime
juice until all are mixed well. Carry in a lidded
plastic container.

SESAME CRISP CANDY

¶ 9 × 13″ pan's worth

Crispy, crunchy, chewy, and sweet.

2 cups sesame seeds
½ cup nuts, chopped
½ cup honey
½ cup brown sugar
1 teaspoon ginger
1 teaspoon cinnamon
4 cardamom pods, husks removed

In a moderate oven (350°), toast the sesame seeds
and nuts for 15 minutes. Meanwhile, in a frying
pan over medium heat melt the honey, sugar, and
spices. Stir constantly, bring to a boil, and cook 2
minutes. Remove from the heat and stir in the
seeds and nuts, mixing well. Turn into an oiled 9
by 13 inch pan and press flat. Cut while slightly
warm. Cool before wrapping.

Variations: Add ½ cup chopped dried fruit; ½ cup
coconut.

SPREADS
AND DRESSINGS

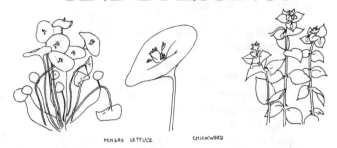

MINERS LETTUCE   CHICKWEED

Prepare these before you go, eliminating
some mess in camp. The spreads are good
for any meal, especially lunch, when you
usually don't want to cook. Toss the
dressings into warm pasta, rice, or bulgar.

HUMUS

■■■

¶ 2 cups

This is a Middle Eastern spread or dip. Carry it in
a plastic tube or a wide-mouth container. Serve on
Journey Cakes or crackers.

1½ cups garbanzo beans
¾ cup sesame tahini
juice of 2 lemons
¼ cup (packed) parsley, chopped fine
¼ cup scallions, minced
3 garlic cloves, crushed
2 teaspoons cumin
1 teaspoon salt
dash of soy sauce
pinch each of black pepper and cayenne pepper

Soak the beans overnight. Cook them until they
are well done (about 1½–2 hours). Add the
remaining ingredients and blend together. Chill.
Carry in a lidded plastic container.

SESAME BUTTER SPREAD

¶ ½ cup

Good spread on crackers.

½ cup raw sesame butter
dash salt
grated orange peel (optional)

Roast the sesame butter and salt in a frying pan
until brown, stirring constantly, about 5–10
minutes in all. Add the orange peel when cool.
Carry in a lidded plastic container.

MISO SPREAD

¶ serves two

Use this as a thin spread on breads or Journey
Cakes, with or without sliced cheese. It's easy to
make in camp, too.

3–4 cloves garlic, minced
2 tablespoons water
1 tablespoon sesame *or* peanut butter
1 teaspoon miso
¼ teaspoon olive oil (enough to just cover bottom
of pan)

Put the oil in a frying pan and add the garlic. Stir
lightly until the garlic turns somewhat translucent. Mix the miso and peanut or sesame butter,
and add them and the water to the pan. Stir until
thick. Carry in a lidded plastic container.

Variations: Serve a small amount of the spread
with rice or another grain for extra flavor and
nourishment.

MISO SESAME BUTTER SPREAD

■■

¶ approximately ¾ cup

This is a high-protein, quick energy spread. It's good for lunch on crackers, cold leftover pancakes, or bread.

¾ cup sesame butter
2 tablespoons miso
2–3 tablespoons boiling water
grated orange peel (optional)

Brown the sesame butter and miso together in a frying pan, stirring constantly. Add water and mix to spreading consistency. Cool and add the orange peel. Carry in a lidded plastic container.

GARLIC SPREAD

■■

¶ approximately ⅓ cup

This spread is good on bread with spaghetti or chili, or alone when you get a garlic craving. It may be made in camp, too.

12–15 large garlic cloves, chopped large
⅓ cup water
1 tablespoon butter *or* olive oil

Combine the water and garlic and bring them to a boil in a saucepan. Lower the heat and simmer for 10–15 minutes. Add the butter or oil and stir well. Carry in a lidded plastic container.

MIXED SEED BUTTER (SWEET)

¶ approximately 1¾ cups

Use this on bread, crackers, sweet Journey Cakes, or add a little more water and spread it on pancakes.

½ cup pumpkin seeds
½ cup sunflower seeds
¼ cup sesame butter
2 tablespoons honey
1 tablespoon oil
1 tablespoon water (approximate)

In a seed grinder or blender, grind the pumpkin and sunflower seeds. Then combine all the ingredients in a bowl and mix well. Store and carry in an airtight plastic container.

Variations: To make a Salty Mixed Seed Butter, follow the same recipe, but replace the honey with 2 teapoons miso and increase the amount of water to approximately 3 tablespoons.

MISO DRESSING

It's easy to mix up a small amount of salad dressing before you go, put it in a jar, and carry it in your pack, ready to use. This recipe has added nourishment because of the miso, and it keeps well.

1 teaspoon each miso, oil, water, and lemon juice
1 clove garlic, sliced
½ teaspoon whole oregano, thyme, *or* basil

Carry in a small airtight bottle, and shake well before using.

SESAME BUTTER DRESSING

Salad dressings taste really good in the mountains. Make a pot of noodles, drain, add lots of dried parsley and onions, remove from the heat, and toss in some dressing. Also use this dressing with boiled or baked potatoes adding some dill or other herbs.

1 tablespoon sesame *or* peanut butter
2–3 tablespoons water
1 teaspoon tamari soy sauce
1 teaspoon lemon juice
½ teaspoon chervil, dill, *or* tarragon

Put all the ingredients in a small airtight bottle. Shake well before using.

MUSTARDY VINAIGRETTE DRESSING

Toss this dressing with warm pasta, rice, bulgar, or fresh grated vegetables.

¼ cup oil
2 tablespoons olive oil
2 tablespoons red wine vinegar
1 shallot *or* onion
4 teaspoons Dijon mustard
⅛ teaspoon tarragon
salt and pepper to taste

Put the ingredients into a blender and blend until smooth. Carry in an airtight plastic bottle. Shake well before using.

LEMON TAHINI DRESSING

Toss with warm pasta, instant wild rice, or cooked mung beans and chopped nuts.

¼ cup lemon juice
3 tablespoons oil
2 tablespoons sesame tahini
1 tablespoon tamari soy sauce
1 tablespoon water
1 garlic clove
pinch each of celery seed, salt, pepper

Put all the ingredients in a blender. Blend until smooth. Carry in an airtight plastic bottle. Shake before using.

FRESH FOODS

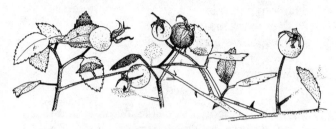

Bring Along:
cucumbers, potatoes, onions,
garlic, cabbage, yams, carrots,
oranges, lemons, apples

A small amount of fresh food is a treat when added to the usual dry diet of backpacking. The foods listed keep well and go a long way. However, for snow camping, we do not recommend taking fresh food along, except for oranges to eat the first day or so.

Take along a small grater for carrots, cabbage, apples, and cucumbers, and add them to salads, soups, and stews. Potatoes are good fried for breakfast with onions and garlic or as an accompaniment to a trout dinner. Bake or boil the potatoes at home, cool, and carry them whole in a plastic bag. In camp, chop them into soups, or marinate them with mixed herbs and a dressing for a delicious salad.

Lemons, onions, and garlic have many possibilities, and we recommend taking lots of them along. If you are carrying water, add a sliced whole lemon to a gallon of water to keep it fresh longer.

Chop up vegetables at home (maybe just the odds and ends left in the refrigerator) and combine them with cheese and herbs. Wrapping them first tightly in foil and then in a plastic bag for a delicious supper to cook the first night in camp.

POTATOES AND MUSHROOMS

¶ serves two
¶ 5–10 minutes

2 cups chopped mushrooms
2 potatoes with skins on, boiled and chopped
1 onion, chopped (optional)
½ cup chopped pecans
2 garlic cloves, sliced
2 tablespoons butter
parsley *or* mixed herbs to taste
salt, pepper to taste
cheddar cheese to taste, grated or cubed

At Home: Combine the ingredients, except the cheese, and place in an airtight zip-locking plastic bag. Dot with butter and seal well.

In Camp: Empty the contents of the bag into a frying pan and cook, covered, over moderate heat for 5–10 minutes. Stir in the cheese and serve.

Variation: Blend in 1 tablespoon of vermouth before packaging.

Two monks, one older than the other, were traveling in a remote mountain region, visiting from temple to temple. They had heard of a great master living in a temple high up on the mountain, and started out on the trail to visit him. Just as they were turning up toward the temple, a lettuce leaf came floating down the creek. The young monk exclaimed at the waste and questioned the greatness of the master. Just as he did so, the tenzo *(head cook) came running down over boulders and grass with beard and robes flying, pursuing the lost lettuce leaf.*

2.

FOODS TO MAKE IN CAMP

Planning and prepackaging individual meals at home before the trip makes each meal simple and quick to prepare in camp and allows you to create a menu that is varied and pure. Remember to adjust cooking times for your particular stove, cookware, and camp elevation.

CEREALS

High-protein grains and protein
combinations, nuts, dried fruit, and butter
all appear in these energizing breakfast
cereal recipes. In winter, when you use
more energy to keep your endurance level
up, you may want to expand your breakfast
with one of the following:

a chunk of cheese while you wait
for the cereal to cook,
nut or seed butters in your
cereal or on your bread,
almond or cashew meal added to
your cereal,
soy, cashew, or almond milk,
extra amounts of dried fruits
and nuts in your cereal,
soy grits or millet
added to the cereal before cooking,
wheat germ and nutritional
yeast added after cooking.

SEED CEREAL

¶ approximately 2½ cups
¶ instant

This is good by itself with cold or warm milk, or served with Stewed Fruit. It may also be used as a high-protein garnish for hot cereals.

1 cup almonds
½ cup pumpkin seeds
½ cup sunflower seeds
¼ cup date sugar
2 tablespoons carob powder (optional)

At Home: Grind the nuts and seeds, and combine them with the remaining ingredients. Store in an airtight container with a lid.

In Camp: Serve as a cereal or use as a topping for hot cereals, soups, stewed fruit, or added nourishment in one-pot meals.

SOAKED CEREAL

▪▪▪

¶ serves two to three
¶ soak overnight

1 cup rolled oats
1 cup rolled wheat
raisins, to taste
coconut, unsweetened, to taste
dried apples, chopped, to taste

At Home: Combine all the ingredients in an airtight zip-locking plastic bag.

In Camp: The night before, empty the contents of the package into your cookpot. Stir in *3 cups* of cold water, cover the pot, and set it aside until the morning. Serve warm or cold. Sweeten to taste.

Variations: Add chopped nuts; add dried apricots, dates, or other fruit; mix ⅔ cup milk powder with water and add; add cinnamon or other spices; try it with rolled barley or rye; add sesame or sunflower seeds.

BIRD SEED CEREAL

This cereal has the unique flavor of raw whole grains. The texture is crunchy and chewy.

¼ cup rolled oats
¼ cup millet
¼ cup milk powder
¼ cup almonds *or* filberts, chopped
2 tablespoons rolled wheat
2 tablespoons toasted buckwheat groats
small handful of raisins, chopped dates, and
    sunflower seeds
pinch salt
date sugar (optional)

At Home: Combine the dry ingredients in a zip-locking plastic bag.

In Camp: The night before, empty the contents of the bag in your cookpot and stir in *1 cup* of water. Cover the pot and set it aside. In the morning serve the cereal cold or warm it up over low heat, stirring frequently.

WHEAT GERM CEREAL

This is a good breakfast cereal to keep you moving.

½ cup raw wheat germ
½ cup bran flakes
¼ teaspoon salt

At Home: Mix the ingredients and place them in an airtight zip-locking plastic bag.

In Camp: Bring 2 *cups* of water to a boil. Stir in the cereal. Cover the pot and remove it from the heat. Let the cereal sit about 5 minutes. Serve hot.

Variations: Serve with honey or dried fruit (dates are especially good); add ½ cup rolled oats and 1 cup more water; add nuts.

COLD MORNING WHEAT CEREAL

■■■

¶ serves two
¶ 5–10 minutes

The dried fruit makes this cereal sweet and the butter helps keep you warm.

1 cup finely cracked wheat *or* bulgar
¼ cup milk powder
½ teaspoon salt
handful of raisins *or* pitted dates
handful of walnuts
2 tablespoons butter

At Home: Combine all the ingredients in a zip-locking plastic bag.

In Camp: Bring *4 cups* water to a boil. Stir in the contents of the bag and return to a boil. Cover the pot, remove it from the heat, and let the cereal sit 5–10 minutes or until tender.

Variations: This can also be made with Bear Mush, a cracked wheat cereal available in natural food stores.

HOT CRACKED MILLET CREAM CEREAL

¶ serves two
¶ 10 minutes

A good winter cereal, high in protein and a source of calcium and iron. It's delicious.

½ cup cracked millet
⅔ cup dates
⅔ cup black walnuts, filberts, *or* almonds,
    chopped large
¼ teaspoon salt
2 teaspoons oil *or* butter (optional)
coconut (optional), unsweetened, to taste

At Home: In a skillet over moderate heat, toast the millet until it's golden brown. Put it in a blender and crack but do not grind it. Let it cool. Then combine it with the remaining ingredients in an airtight zip-locking bag.

In Camp: Bring *2 cups* of water to a boil. Slowly stir in the contents of the bag. Cook 8–10 minutes, stirring frequently.

BULGAR CORNMEAL CEREAL

■■

¶ serves two
¶ 5–10 minutes

⅓ cup cornmeal
¼ cup bulgar
⅓ cup chopped dried apricots or peaches
    or currants or raisins
¼ teaspoon salt
1 tablespoon butter

TOPPING
1 tablespoon toasted sesame seeds
1 tablespoon date sugar
⅛ teaspoon cinnamon

At Home: Package the cereal and topping ingredients separately in two zip-locking plastic bags.

In Camp: Bring *1⅔ cups* water to a boil. Stir in the contents of the bag, and bring back to a boil. Then reduce the heat and simmer 5 minutes, stirring frequently. When cooked, sprinkle on the topping and serve.

RICE CREAM CEREAL

¶ serves two
¶ 5 minutes

A delicate cereal that's good for small children.
Serve with butter and honey.

½ cup brown rice flour, toasted

At Home: In a skillet over moderate heat, toast the
flour until it's golden brown. Cool and package in
a zip-locking plastic bag.

In Camp: Empty the contents of the bag into your
cookpot. Stir in 2 *cups* of water, bring to a boil,
and cook for 5 minutes.

OATS AND GROATS

¶ serves two
¶ 15 minutes

½ cup rolled oats
½ cup toasted buckwheat groats
½ cup (approximately) chopped dried apricots
honey, to taste
butter, to taste

At Home: Combine all the ingredients in an airtight
zip-locking bag.

In Camp: Empty the contents of the bag into your
cookpot. Stir in 3 *cups* of water and bring to a boil.
Reduce the heat, cover the pot, and simmer 15
minutes. To reduce the cooking time, soak the
cereal from 1 hour to overnight.

PANCAKES

Pancakes are good on slow mornings, when
you feel like sitting in the sun
on a granite boulder with a cup of hot
tea, letting it all soak in and warm you
after a frosty night. Cook extra and serve
them as bread for lunch.

OATMEAL HOTCAKES

¶ serves two
¶ soak 10 minutes

These are good on those mornings when you want to eat a lot. They are sweet and filling.

2 cups oatmeal
½ cup milk powder
¼ teaspoon cinnamon
¼ teaspoon nutmeg
¼ teaspoon salt
¼ cup date sugar (optional)
¼ cup currants *or* raisins
1 tablespoon sesame seeds
1 teaspoon baking powder
2 tablespoons oil
1 egg (optional)

At Home: Whir the oatmeal in a blender or processor until most of it is a flourlike consistency. Leave some in small pieces. Then combine with the dry ingredients and package in an airtight zip-locking plastic bag.

In Camp: Add optional egg, the oil and 1¼ *cups* of water. Let the mixture stand at least 10 minutes before gently cooking the pancakes to a golden brown. Serve with butter and honey. Leftovers are great to snack on.

CORN PANCAKES

These are good with peanut butter and maple syrup or Stewed Fruit.

¾ cup corn flour or cornmeal
¾ cup whole wheat flour
½ cup raw wheat germ
½ cup milk powder
2 teaspoons baking powder
½ teaspoon salt
2 tablespoons oil *or* butter
1 tablespoon honey (optional)

At Home: Combine all the ingredients in a zip-locking plastic bag.

In Camp: Empty the contents of the bag into a pot or bowl. Stir in *1½ cups* water. Cook on a hot oiled pan. Save leftovers for lunch.

WHOLE WHEAT SOY PANCAKES

¶ serves two

These are good, heavy pancakes, very high in protein and energy. They come out dark and are delicious with maple syrup.

2 cups whole wheat flour
½ cup soy flour
½ cup raw wheat germ
½ cup milk powder
2 teaspoons baking powder
1 teaspoon salt
2 tablespoons oil

At Home: Combine all the ingredients in a ziplocking plastic bag.

In Camp: Empty the contents of the bag into a bowl or pot. Stir in *2 cups* of water. Cook the cakes on a hot oiled pan.

BROWN RICE FLOUR PANCAKES

■■

¶ serves two

Light, mellow pancakes. They are good with
sesame butter and honey or maple syrup.

2 cups brown rice flour
⅓ cup milk powder
2 teaspoons baking powder
½ teaspoon salt
2 tablespoons honey
2 tablespoons oil

At Home: Combine all the ingredients in an airtight
zip-locking plastic bag.

In Camp: Add *1 cup* of water to the pancake mix
and stir. Cook the cakes on a hot oiled pan.

BUCKWHEAT PANCAKES

■■

¶ serves two to four

1 cup buckwheat flour
½ cup whole wheat flour
½ cup cornmeal
½ cup raw wheat germ
½ cup milk powder
2 teaspoons baking powder
1 teaspoon salt
2 tablespoons oil

At Home: Package all the ingredients together in a
zip-locking plastic bag.

In Camp: Empty the contents of the bag into a
bowl or pot. Stir in *2–3 cups* of water. Cook the
pancakes on a hot oiled pan.

Variations: Add raisins, or dried bananas, chopped
small.

BREADS TO MAKE IN CAMP

Fresh bread in camp after a few days of backpacking is a real treat. Bake extra for lunches or breakfast.

Care must be taken when baking pan breads on a fuel stove, as the heat is fierce and the bread will easily scorch. Using a thick-bottomed pan or a heat diffuser between the pan and the stove and keeping the heat down will prevent this.

If fresh baked bread in camp is something you enjoy often while backpacking, Optimus offers a "mini-oven" that bakes breads, cakes, and casseroles over a camp stove.

We have included two steamed bread recipes that take a while to cook, but are wonderfully moist and tender.

CORNBREAD

¶ serves four or two with leftovers
¶ 30–40 minutes

Everybody likes cornbread, hot from the pan.
Serve it with maple syrup for breakfast, smothered
in chili for supper, dripping with butter and honey
for dessert, or cold with peanut butter or cheese
for lunch. Use the longer cooking time if you are
at 8,000 feet or over.

¾ cup cornmeal
¾ cup whole wheat flour
⅓ cup raw wheat germ
3 tablespoons buttermilk powder
1½ teaspoons baking powder
½ teaspoon baking soda
2 tablespoons honey
¼ cup minus 1 tablespoon of oil

At Home: Combine all the dry ingredients in an
airtight zip-locking plastic bag. Pour the honey
and oil into a capped plastic bottle.

In Camp: Add the honey and oil with ¾ *cup* of
water to the dry ingredients. Mix to combine. Pour
into a greased pan, cover, and steam for 30–40
minutes (use the steaming instructions on page
22). The bread will be springy to the touch. Cover
again and steam an extra 10 minutes if necessary.

Alternately, you can use a frying pan with a lid,
with a heat diffuser between the pan and the flame.
Cook for 20 minutes, then flip the bread over to
complete cooking. This method has to be watched
carefully as a thin pan and a fierce flame will burn
the bread's bottom before it is cooked.

Variations: Use one of the following: 2 teaspoons
cumin; or ½ cup fresh Parmesan cheese; or chili
flakes; or nuts and seeds.

WHOLE WHEAT IRISH SODA BREAD

¶ serves two
¶ 20 minutes

¾ cup whole wheat flour
2 tablespoons buttermilk powder
½ teaspoon baking soda
½ teaspoon baking powder

At Home: Package all the ingredients together in an airtight zip-locking plastic bag.

In Camp: Add ½ *cup* of water to the dry ingredients and mix well. Drop the dough onto an oiled thick-bottomed pan or use a heat diffuser. Use the stove's lowest heat, turning after the bottom has firmed up. Turn it several times. A lid on the pan will make the bread cook a little faster. The bread will take about 20 minutes and will sound hollow when you tap the crust.

Variations: Use half unbleached white, half whole wheat flour; add 1 tablespoon of dried mixed herbs; add a handful of dried fruit or raisins.

SINGING HINNIES

This is a country recipe from the British Isles. It got it's name from the sizzling butter, which was thought to be singing.

1 cup unbleached flour *or* whole wheat flour
¼ cup brown rice flour
¼ cup milk powder
1 teaspoon baking powder
3 tablespoons butter
handful of raisins
extra flour

At Home: Sift together the dry ingredients. Rub in the butter and add the raisins. Package in an air-tight zip-locking plastic bag. Package a little (2 tablespoons) extra flour separately.

In Camp: Add ½ *cup* of water to the dry ingredients, combine well, and pat into four flat disks about half an inch thick. Dust your hands with a little of the extra flour so you don't get sticky.

Heat a thick-bottomed pan (or use a heat diffuser) over moderate heat, drop the Hinnies, and cook, turning once, for about 15 minutes. They will cook a little quicker with a lid on. Watch that flame— keep it as low as possible!

Eat well buttered and save the extras for lunch.

DROP SCONES

¶ serves two to four
¶ 5–10 minutes

A Scottish favorite for tea. Serve them as a bread
with dinner and bake extras for lunch. There are
many variations, sweet to savory.

½ cup whole wheat flour
½ cup unbleached white flour
2 tablespoons buttermilk powder
2 teaspoons baking powder
1 tablespoon butter
1 egg (optional)
¾–1 cup water

At Home: Combine all the dry ingredients and rub
in the butter. Package in a zip-locking plastic bag.

In Camp: Add the egg and enough water to make a
thick batter. Drop from a spoon onto a slightly
greased hot frying pan. When puffed and full of
bubbles, turn and brown the other side.

Variations: Add one of the following: 2 teaspoons
dried mixed herbs; ½ cup Parmesan cheese; ½
cup currants; 1 teaspoon mixed spices (cinnamon,
nutmeg, and so on); 2 teaspoons curry powder;
grated orange or lemon rind; a slice of cheese on
the top before turning.

WHOLE WHEAT BREAD

¶ serves two to four
¶ cooking time: 10–30 minutes

This is a luxury bread for long trips; leftovers for lunch if you can stop eating it. The bread will rise as you hike.

1½ cups whole wheat flour
¼ cup raw wheat germ
pinch salt
1 tablespoon dry yeast
1 tablespoon molasses *or* honey
1 cup warm water

At Home: In a sturdy, airtight, 1 gallon plastic bag, combine the flour, wheat germ, salt, and yeast. Carry the molasses or honey in an airtight plastic bottle.

In Camp: Add the molasses and cup of lukewarm water to the bag of flour mixture; mix them together by stirring in the bag or by squeezing the mixture through the plastic until it is well blended. Twist-tie the bag, leaving plenty of air space for the bread to expand. Place the dough in your pack carefully, or it could be a real mess. Leave it to rise a few hours to all day. At the end of the day, knead the dough and form it into a round loaf.

There are three methods of baking:
Oil or dust with flour a thick-bottomed pan and place the loaf in it. Cover the loaf with a bandana or plastic bag, and let it rise again in the sunshine for 20 minutes. If the sun is down, warm the pan first and let the dough sit in the warm covered pan. Cook over low heat, turning, for about 15–20 minutes or until it sounds hollow when you tap the crust.

Cook as individual Drop Scones (page 102). Cook

on an oiled pan for 10–15 minutes.

Steam the bread (follow directions on page 22), after letting the dough rise in the steaming bowl for 20 minutes in a warm spot. (To rise the dough, warm the water, and place the bowl in it.) After the dough rises, bring the water to a boil; start timing after it comes to a boil. It will take 30 minutes—the top will be springy to the touch. This is by far the most successful method.

RYE BATTER BREAD

¶ 4 large servings
¶ 20–40 minutes

This bread can be made with many variations to suit your taste buds. The recipe is large enough for dinner and lunch the next day; halve it if you want to reduce cooking time.

2 cups rye flour
1 cup whole wheat flour
pinch salt
2 teaspoons baking soda
6 tablespoons buttermilk powder
1–3 tablespoons molasses, depending on sweet-
    ness desired
    oil *or* butter
    flavorings:
    2 tablespoons dried onion and 2 teaspoons
    dried dill *or* 2 teaspoons carraway seed *or*
    fennel seed *or* 2 teaspoons dried orange peel
    and 1 teaspoon crushed cardamom *or* ½ cup
    dried raisins and 1 teaspoon cinnamon *or* ½
    cup grated Parmesan cheese and 2 table-
    spoons dried pepper flakes

At Home: Package all the dry ingredients together in an airtight zip-locking plastic bag. Add your choice of one of the flavorings to the bag. Combine the oil and molasses in a plastic bottle with a lid.

In Camp: Add 1 ⅔ *cups* of water and the molasses mixture to the dry ingredients and mix to combine. Don't overmix or you will toughen the dough. Pour into an oiled pan and bake without delay for 20–40 minutes depending on your cooking method.

¶ Steam according to the steaming directions on page 22 for 40 minutes or until the bread is springy to the touch.

¶ Bake in an oiled frying pan using a heat diffuser between the flame and the pan. Flip to bake the other side when the top begins to set after about 30 minutes.

¶ Bake in a stove-top oven such as the mini-oven Optimus puts out. Baking time is about 20 minutes.

SOUPS

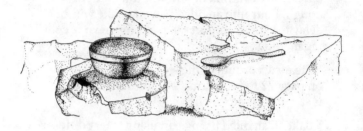

We have found that it's easy and satisfying to package our own soup mixes—controlling what goes in them, keeping the cost down, and making taste changes and nutritional supplements. All of these soups are quick and easy to make. Just add water in camp. Serve them as a light meal, with a bread or Journey Cake for a complete meal, or as an accompaniment to the main course.

GARLIC BROTH

¶ 1 quart
¶ 15 minutes or longer

This is basic and nourishing broth, easy and inexpensive to make. It's fine the way it is or with a little Parmesan cheese sprinkled on top. It's also a good base for soup or stew or for cooking dumplings. Try it with a fresh potato cooked in it. Or rice, lentils, croutons, . . .

20–30 garlic cloves, crushed
2 tablespoons parsley flakes
1 teaspoon sage
1 teaspoon thyme
1 whole clove
1 small bay leaf
2 tablespoons olive oil (optional)

At Home: Combine and package all the ingredients in a zip-locking plastic bag.

In Camp: Add the ingredients to *1 quart* of water. Bring to a boil, reduce the heat, and simmer covered for 15 minutes or longer. Sprinkle on Sesame Salt.

HERB VEGETABLE BROTH

¶ serves two
¶ 5 minutes

Use this broth to simmer dumplings, noodles, Chinese bean threads, or serve it as a cup of broth.

1 vegetable bouillon cube *or* 1 tablespoon
      bouillon powder
2 tablespoons dried mushrooms, chopped fine
2 tablespoons dried chives
1 tablespoon mixed dried herbs
2 garlic cloves, crushed
4 sundried tomatoes, chopped

At Home: Package all ingredients in a zip-locking plastic bag.

In Camp: Empty the contents of the bag into a cookpot and stir in *4 cups* of water. Bring to a boil, cover, and simmer 3–5 minutes.

Variations: Add a fresh grated carrot and/or a chopped onion.

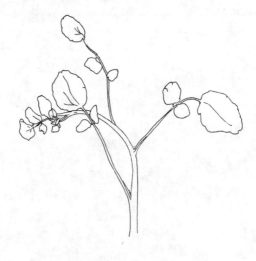

MISO SOUP

¶ serves two
¶ 5 minutes

Miso is worth its weight in gold. It can make a complete meal or be a very good hot broth by itself for quick energy. Good for breakfast, too.

4 by 4 inch piece of kombu (seaweed)
3 tablespoons dried fish flakes *or* handful iriki (small dried fish)
2 tablespoons miso
2 teaspoons tamari soy sauce
1 teaspoon toasted sesame oil

At Home: Combine the seaweed and fish flakes in an airtight plastic bag. Package the miso, oil, and soy sauce separately.

In Camp: Bring *4 cups* of water to a boil. Stir in the seaweed mixture and boil for 5 minutes. Stir in the miso mixture, heat thoroughly, and serve.

Variations: Add 8 ounces of noodles at the beginning; drop in Dilly Dumplings at the beginning and cook 10 minutes in all; add dried shrimp at the beginning, or canned fish or shrimp at the end.

Garnishes: Sliced lemon; broken pieces of Zwieback; popcorn; dried chives; Parmesan cheese.

FISH SOUP

This is a nice change from steamed or fried fish.
Use a fillet of fresh fish. Or else use canned fish.

6 ounces noodles: spinach, whole wheat,
   or vegironi
1 bay leaf
1 vegetable bouillon cube *or* 1 tablespoon
   vegetable bouillon powder *or* 1
   tablespoon
   mixed dried herbs
pinch of black pepper
1 cup fresh fish fillet *or* 1 can tuna or other
   seafood

At Home: Package all the ingredients together,
except the fish, in a zip-locking plastic bag.

In Camp: Bring *4 cups* of water to a boil. Stir in the
noodle mixture and boil for 5 minutes. Then stir
in the fresh filleted fish and cook an additional 5
minutes. If you are using canned fish, stir it in
when the noodles are cooked.

KOMBU FISH BROTH

This is a good salty broth for a strenuous day. It may be served as is or with enough additions to make a complete meal.

4 by 4 inch piece of kombu (seaweed)
3 tablespoons bonita fish flakes *or* handful of
    iriki (small dried fish)
¼ cup tamari soy sauce

At Home: Package all the ingredients except the tamari in a zip-locking plastic bag. Carry the soy sauce in a lidded plastic bottle.

In Camp: Bring *4 cups* of water to a boil. Lower the heat, add the seaweed and fish, and simmer 10–15 minutes. Strain (optional). Add the tamari.

Garnishes: Toasted sesame seeds; Parmesan cheese; popcorn.

Variations: Ingredients from Seaweed Soup; drop in Dilly Dumplings after the broth comes to a boil; add handful of dried shrimp at the beginning or freeze-dried or canned shrimp at the end; add 6 ounces of noodles when the broth comes to a boil.

SEAWEED SOUP

Served with Sesame Seed Bread with a nut or seed butter spread on top.

4 by 4 inch piece of kombu (seaweed)
¼ cup hiziki (seaweed)
¼ cup dried shredded daikon (white radish) (optional)
3 tablespoons bonita fish flakes
2 tablespoons dried mushrooms, sliced thin and chopped fine
1 tablespoon onion flakes
¼ teaspoon ginger, ground
handful dried shrimp

At Home: Combine all the ingredients in an airtight zip-locking plastic bag.

In Camp: Combine all the ingredients in a cookpot with *5 cups* of water and bring to a boil. Then keep at high simmer for 25–30 minutes. Sprinkle sesame seeds or onion slices on top.

PARTAN BREE

¶ serves two
¶ 5–10 minutes

A mild, milky Scottish soup, light in flavor, for one of those nights when you need something soothing to eat.

½ cup milk powder
¼ cup oats
2 tablespoons dried chives
1 teaspoon parsley flakes
¼ teaspoon salt
¼ teaspoon nutmeg
2 tablespoons butter (optional)
pepper to taste
1 6½-ounce can crabmeat with juice

At Home: Package all the dry ingredients together in a zip-locking plastic bag. Carry the crab and butter separately.

In Camp: Place the dry ingredients in a cookpot and slowly add *4 cups* of water. Bring to a boil, stirring constantly. Cover, and reduce the heat. Simmer 5–10 minutes. Remove from the heat and stir in the crab and the optional butter. Reheat and serve.

SPINACH CLAM SOUP

¶ serves two
¶ 3–5 minutes

½ cup dehydrated spinach
1 teaspoon onion flakes *or* 1 fresh onion,
    chopped in camp
1 teaspoon parsley flakes
¼ teaspoon garlic granules *or* 2 fresh garlic
    cloves, crushed in camp
1 teaspoon basil
dash nutmeg
dash pepper
1 6½-ounce can clams and juice
Parmesan cheese and/or chopped almonds
    as garnish

At Home: Package all the ingredients together
in a zip-locking plastic bag. Package the garnish
separately.

In Camp: Place the ingredients in a cookpot and
slowly add *3½ cups* of water. Bring to a boil, stirring constantly. Reduce the heat, cover, and simmer for 3 minutes. Remove from the heat, stir in
the clams, and reheat. Sprinkle cheese or nuts on
top to serve.

MINESTRONE

½ cup freeze-dried navy, pinto, *or* kidney beans
(optional)
¼ cup broken spaghetti
¼ cup Parmesan cheese, grated
2 tablespoons tomato powder *or* vegetable
bouillon cube
2 tablespoons parsley flakes
1 tablespoon dehydrated spinach flakes (optional)
1 tablespoon onion flakes *or* 1 small fresh onion,
chopped in camp
1 tablespoon celery flakes
1 tablespoon dried bell pepper (optional)
1–2 teaspoons basil
1 teaspoon oregano
½ teaspoon salt and pepper
1 garlic clove, minced in camp, *or* ⅛ teaspoon
garlic granules

At Home: Package the ingredients together in a
zip-locking plastic bag.

In Camp: Place the ingredients in a cookpot and
slowly add *4 cups* of water. Bring to a boil, stirring
constantly. Reduce heat, cover, and simmer 5–10
minutes or until the noodles and beans are tender.

SALSA SOUP WITH CORN CHEESE DUMPLINGS

¶ serves two
¶ 10–15 minutes

Olé!

¼ cup tomato powder
2 tablespoons dried onion *or* 1 fresh onion,
     chopped in camp
2 tablespoons dried bell pepper
2 garlic cloves, minced in camp, *or* ¼ teaspoon
     garlic granules or powder
1–3 teaspoons dried cilantro
1 teaspoon dried oregano
1 teaspoon cumin seeds, ground
½ teaspoon red chili powder
Corn Cheese Dumplings

At Home: Combine all the ingredients, and package them in a zip-locking plastic bag.

In Camp: Empty the contents of the bag into a cookpot and slowly stir in *4 cups* of water. Stirring constantly, bring to a boil over moderate heat. Reduce the heat to a simmer, and drop in the dumplings. Cover the pot. Do not peek or lift the lid for 10 minutes. The dumplings will be puffed and springy to the touch. If necessary, cook 5 minutes more.

If you are making soup without the dumplings, after bringing to a boil, cover the pot and simmer 5–10 minutes.

SPICED TOMATO MILLET SOUP

This is an exotic, flavorful soup. Serve it with pocket bread or Potato Cakes for a full meal.

⅓ cup millet
3 tablespoons tomato powder
2 garlic cloves, minced in camp, *or* ½ teaspoon
    garlic granules or powder
1 teaspoon coriander seeds
½ teaspoon fennel seeds
½ teaspoon cardamom seeds
½ teaspoon fenugreek seeds
½ teaspoon tumeric
pinch cayenne
salt to taste

At Home: In a dry skillet over moderate heat, toast the millet. Stir occasionally. When cool, crack it in a blender. Grind all the seeds with a mortar and pestle, a coffee grinder, or electric mill. Combine all the ingredients in an airtight zip-locking plastic bag.

In Camp: In a cookpot, bring 4 *cups* of water to a boil. Stir in the contents of the bag, reduce the heat, cover the pot, and simmer 10–15 minutes.

SPICY HOT AND SOUR SOUP

¶ serves two
¶ 5 minutes

This is a delightful, tasty soup. It has an authentic flavor for Chinese-food lovers. Serve it with Oriental Rice Cakes, Soybean Burgers, or over a bowl of boiled noodles.

2 tablespoons white, rice, *or* cider vinegar
2 tablespoons tamari soy sauce
2 tablespoons rice wine *or* cooking sherry
1 tablespoon cornstarch *or* arrowroot powder
2 teaspoons toasted sesame oil
1 vegetable bouillon cube *or* 1 tablespoon
    vegetable bouillon powder
1 teaspoon fresh ginger, grated
6 Chinese black mushrooms, minced
1–2 eggs beaten (optional)

At Home: Combine all the ingredients except the mushrooms and eggs in a plastic bottle with a lid. Remove the woody stems from the mushrooms and finely chop the tops. Package them in an airtight zip-locking plastic bag. Carry the eggs whole in an egg container.

In Camp: In a cookpot, soak the mushrooms in water to cover for 30 minutes. Stir in the bottled ingredients and add *4 cups* of water. Over moderate heat, bring the soup to a boil, cover the pot, reduce the heat, and cook 3–5 minutes, stirring occasionally. In a bowl, beat the eggs together with a fork until well combined. Give the soup a stir, and pour in the eggs as the soup bubbles. Stir well. This will make egg "threads." Serve immediately.

FIVE-GRAIN SOUP

¶ serves two
¶ 5–10 minutes

This is a filling, creamy soup, and quick-cooking. It's very good for rainy-day lunch in the tent. Serve it with cheese or peanut butter and crackers. It's good with Journey Cakes, too.

3 tablespoons rolled oats
2 tablespoons dehydrated diced potato *or* 1 baked potato, chopped small
1 tablespoon whole wheat flour
1 tablespoon barley flour
1 tablespoon millet flour
1 tablespoon rye flour
1 tablespoon nutritional yeast (optional)
1 tablespoon milk powder
1 tablespoon dehydrated carrots *or* 1 fresh carrot, finely chopped in camp
1 teaspoon onion flakes *or* 1 fresh onion, chopped in camp
1 teaspoon parsley flakes
½ teaspoon salt
dash garlic granules *or* 1 fresh clove garlic, chopped in camp

At Home: Package all the ingredients together in a zip-locking plastic bag.

In Camp: Empty the ingredients into a cookpot and slowly add *4 cups* of water. Stirring constantly, bring to a boil, cover, and reduce the heat, and simmer 5–10 minutes.

SPINACH CHEESE SOUP

¶ serves two
¶ 3–5 minutes

This recipe serves two for lunch or before a main course for supper. Doubled, it serves two for supper along with bread or Journey Cakes.

½ cup milk powder
2 tablespoons whole wheat flour
2 tablespoons spinach flakes
1 onion, chopped in camp, *or* 1 tablespoon dried onion flakes
1 tablespoon parsley flakes (optional)
¼ teaspoon salt
pinch cayenne
1 garlic clove, crushed in camp, *or* ⅛ teaspoon garlic granules
4 ounces cheddar cheese, grated or diced, *or* 1 cup Parmesan, grated
handful of toasted chopped almonds (optional)
2 tablespoons vermouth (optional)

At Home: Package the cheese separately. Put all the dry ingredients into a zip-locking plastic bag. Carry the vermouth in a plastic bottle.

In Camp: Put the dry ingredients in a cookpot, and slowly add 3 *cups* of water. Stirring constantly, bring to a boil, cover, and reduce the heat to a simmer for 3–5 minutes. Remove the pot from the heat, and stir in the cheese and vermouth.

POTATO CHEESE SOUP

This is a thick, filling soup.

½ cup dehydrated potato pieces *or* 1 unpeeled
    baked potato, chopped small
½ cup milk powder
2 tablespoons oats
2 tablespoons whole wheat flour
1 tablespoon onion flakes *or* 1 fresh onion,
    chopped in camp
1 tablespoon raw wheat germ
1 glove garlic, minced in camp
1 teaspoon parsley flakes
1 teaspoon dill weed (optional)
½ teaspoon salt
dash pepper and nutmeg
½ pound cheddar cheese, cut in chunks,
    or ¼ pound Parmesan, grated

At Home: Package the cheese separately. Package
the other ingredients together in a zip-locking
plastic bag.

In Camp: Empty the ingredients into a cookpot
and slowly add *4 cups* of water. Bring to a boil,
stirring constantly. Cover, and reduce the heat to a
simmer for 3–5 minutes. Remove from the heat
and stir in the cheese.

MINTED CREAM OF PEA SOUP

¶ serves two
¶ 5–10 minutes

This is a delicate, light soup, with a fresh pea flavor, perfumed with mint. Serve it as a light snack with steamed Cornbread or crackers and cheese.

½ cup milk powder
2 ounces freeze-dried peas
3 tablespoons whole wheat flour
2 tablespoons dried chives
1 tablespoon dried mint
¼ teaspoon nutmeg
2 garlic cloves, minced in camp, *or* ¼ teaspoon
    garlic granules *or* ½ teaspoon garlic powder
salt and pepper to taste

At Home: Combine all the ingredients in a zip-locking plastic bag.

In Camp: Empty the contents of the bag into a cookpot. Slowly stir in *4 cups* of water. Bring to a boil, cover the pot, reduce the heat, and simmer for 3–5 minutes. Stir occasionally to prevent sticking.

CREAM OF TOMATO SOUP

¶ serves two
¶ 3–5 minutes

This is a light soup for lunch or before dinner. For a complete meal, add a can of seafood or some cubed cheese. Serve with steamed Cornbread or Potato Cake.

½ cup milk powder
¼ cup tomato powder
3 tablespoons whole wheat flour
1 tablespoon dried chives
2 teaspoons basil
2 garlic cloves, minced in camp, *or* ¼ teaspoon
    garlic granules *or* ½ teaspoon garlic powder
4 sundried tomatoes, chopped
pinch of cayenne
½ teaspoon salt

At Home: Package all the ingredients together in a zip-locking plastic bag.

In Camp: Empty the contents of the bag into a cookpot. Slowly stir in *4 cups* of water. Stir over moderate heat, and bring to a boil. Cover the pot, reduce the heat, and simmer, stirring occasionally, for 3–5 minutes.

Variations: Add one of the following: 1 teaspoon dried orange rind; 1 tablespoon mint *or* mixed herbs; *or* 1 tablespoon curry powder and shredded apple.

CREAM OF CELERY SOUP

¶ serves two
¶ 3–5 minutes

This is a thick soup, like a chowder. Light celery flavor. Good with Journey Cakes or Herbed Drop Scones.

½ cup mashed potato powder *or* 3 tablespoons
    whole wheat flour
½ cup milk powder
4 tablespoons celery flakes
1 tablespoon onion flakes *or* 1 fresh onion,
    chopped in camp
1 garlic clove, crushed in camp, *or* ⅛ teaspoon
    garlic granules *or* ¼ teaspoon garlic powder
½ teaspoon salt
¼ teaspoon black pepper
pinch nutmeg
½ cup Parmesan cheese, grated (optional)

At Home: Combine all the ingredients except the cheese in a zip-locking plastic bag. Package the cheese separately.

In Camp: Empty the contents of the bag into a cookpot. Slowly stir in *4 cups* of water. Bring to a boil over moderate heat stirring frequently. Reduce the heat, cover the pot, and cook 3–5 minutes. Stir in the Parmesan cheese and serve.

CREAM OF MUSHROOM SOUP

¶ serves two
¶ 5–10 minutes

A good winter soup. It has a strong mushroom flavor and is thick and creamy.

⅓ cup dried mushrooms, chopped fine
⅓ cup milk powder
2 tablespoons whole wheat flour
2 teaspoons nutritional yeast (optional)
2 teaspoons raw wheat germ
1 teaspoon onion flakes *or* 1 fresh onion,
     chopped in camp
1 teaspoon parsley flakes
½ teaspoon salt
1 clove garlic, minced in camp, *or* ⅛ teaspoon
     garlic granules *or* ¼ teaspoon garlic powder
dash nutmeg
dash pepper

At Home: Package the ingredients together in a zip-locking plastic bag.

In Camp: Empty the bag into a cookpot. Slowly add *4 cups* of water. Bring to a boil, stirring constantly. Reduce the heat, cover the pot, and simmer for 5–10 minutes.

NUT BUTTER SOUP

¶ serves two
¶ 5 minutes

This is great with Cornbread.

½ cup milk powder
2 tablespoons whole wheat flour
1 tablespoon onion flakes *or* 1 fresh onion,
    chopped in camp
½ teaspoon salt
¼ teaspoon celery seeds
¼ teaspoon pepper
1 bay leaf
½ cup peanut, almond, or cashew butter
2 tablespoons Parmesan cheese, grated (optional)

At Home: Combine the dry ingredients in a zip-locking plastic bag. Carry the nut butter and cheese separately.

In Camp: Place the dry ingredients in a cookpot, and slowly add 4 *cups* of water. Bring to a boil, stirring constantly. Cover the pot, reduce the heat, and simmer for 5 minutes. Remove from the heat, and stir in the nut butter and cheese.

CLAM CHOWDER

¶ serves two
¶ 5–10 minutes

½ cup dehydrated diced potato *or* 1 baked
    unpeeled potato, chopped very small in camp
¼ cup milk powder
2 tablespoons whole wheat flour
1 tablespoon celery flakes
1 teaspoon dill weed
¼ teaspoon salt
¼ teaspoon black pepper
1 garlic clove, minced in camp, *or* ⅛ teaspoon
    garlic granules *or* ¼ teaspoon garlic powder.
1 6½-ounce can minced clams with juice

At Home: Package all the ingredients, except
the canned clams, together in a zip-locking
plastic bag.

In Camp: Empty the bag into a cookpot, and slowly
add *4 cups* of water. Stirring constantly, bring to a
boil. Cover the pot, reduce the heat, and simmer
for 3–5 minutes. Cook a further 5 minutes if you're
using fresh potato. Stir in the clams and their
juice; reheat if necessary.

CORN CHOWDER (CRAB OPTIONAL)

This is a thick, creamy chowder. It's high in protein and a special treat with the added crab.

½ cup dehydrated corn
½ cup freeze-dried potatoes *or* 1 unpeeled baked
     potato, cut in small pieces in camp
2 tablespoons cornmeal
2 tablespoons whole wheat flour
2 tablespoons milk powder
1 teaspoon parsley flakes
1 teaspoon onion flakes *or* 1 fresh onion,
     minced in camp
1 teaspoon celery flakes
1 teaspoon dill, thyme, *or* savory
½ teaspoon salt
½ teaspoon paprika
dash pepper
1 tablespoon butter
1 6½-ounce can cracked crab and juice (optional)

At Home: Combine all the ingredients, except the crab, in a zip-locking plastic bag.

In Camp: Empty the bag into a cookpot. Slowly stir in *4½ cups* of water. Over moderate heat, bring to a boil, stirring. Reduce the heat and simmer covered for 10 minutes. Add the crab, heat through, and serve.

PATTIES
AND DUMPLINGS

A bowl of soup topped with dumplings or accompanied by a patty, made fresh in camp, makes a satisfying, complete meal. Patties are also good smothered with a sauce, spread, or gravy.

When adding dumplings to a thick soup, like a chowder, reduce the thickening in the soup by one-half.

MEAL CAKES

¶ serves two
¶ 30 minutes

These cakes will form a brown crust on the outside and inside will slightly steam. Very satisfying in cold weather for breakfast or any time as a dessert after a light supper.

½ cup whole wheat flour
½ cup corn grits
½ cup sunflower seeds, ground
½ cup almonds, ground
¼ teaspoon salt

At Home: Grind the seeds and nuts in a blender, processor, or coffee grinder. Pack the ingredients together in a zip-locking plastic bag.

In Camp: Place the ingredients in a bowl. Add *1 cup* of hot water, stir, and let stand for 15 minutes or so. Take a heaping tablespoon, form a ball (the dough will be moist), and pat into a pancake shape, about ½ inch thick. Cook on a lightly greased pan for 10–15 minutes. Serve with butter and honey or Date Walnut Topping.

These are very good cold for later in the day with peanut butter and honey or a cold topping.

For supper, add:

1 medium onion, chopped fine in camp, *or*
      1 tablespoon onion flakes
1 teaspoon savory *or* your favorite herb
½ teaspoon salt (rather than ¼ teaspoon salt)

Cook as above. Serve with tamari soy sauce, Nut Butter sauce, or Toasted Cashew Ginger Sauce.

FISH PATTIES

serves two
10–15 minutes

1 9¼-ounce can tuna or albacore or other
    canned fish (oil pack), *or* 1½ cups left-
    over cooked fish
¼ cup raw wheat germ
¼ cup milk powder
1 teaspoon dill weed
1 tablespoon oil, if using leftover fish
    (carry separately)
extra raw wheat germ for coating

At Home: Package the dry ingredients together in a
zip-locking plastic bag.

In Camp: Drain the oil from the canned fish into a
pan. Mix the fish with the other ingredients and *1
tablespoon* of water. Form into patties, and coat
with the extra wheat germ. Drop the patties into
hot oil and fry slowly on both sides, about 10–15
minutes. Serve with Sweet and Sour Sauce, Curry
Sauce, or Miso Mustard Sauce.

Variations: Add leftover cooked grain to these patties and they will serve four. Simply double the
dill, add ¼ teaspoon salt, and another tablespoon
of water (depending on the moistness of the
grain). Cook as above (you may need to use more
oil), and serve with soy sauce or mustard. Add 1
tablespoon curry powder to the dry ingredients.

SESAME SEED PATTIES

¶ serves two
¶ 14 minutes

These are tasty, crunchy patties. They are good with a sauce, gravy, hot mustard, or just soy sauce.

1 cup sesame seed meal (ground in a grinder
    or blender)
¼ cup soy flour
¼ cup raw wheat germ
1 teaspoon onion flakes
1 teaspoon parsley flakes
1 teaspoon sage
¼ teaspoon garlic granules *or* ½ teaspoon
    garlic powder
½ teaspoon celery seeds
¼ teaspoon salt
oil for sautéing (carry separately)

At Home: Combine all the ingredients in a zip-locking plastic bag.

In Camp: Add ⅓ *cup* of water to the mixture in the bag and squeeze the bag to mix well. Form into patties and sauté about 7 minutes per side.

SUNFLOWER SEED PATTIES

¶ serves two
¶ 10–15 minutes

These have a mild sunflower seed flavor. They are
very good with Curry or Mushroom Sauce.

1 cup raw sunflower seeds, ground
2 tablespoons whole wheat flour
1 teaspoon celery flakes
1 teaspoon parsley flakes
½ teaspoon chervil
¼ teaspoon salt
¼ teaspoon savory
⅛ teaspoon garlic granules (optional)
Oil for frying (carry separately)

At Home: Package all the ingredients together in a
zip-locking plastic bag.

In Camp: Leave the ingredients in the plastic bag
and add 2–3 *tablespoons* of water. Squeeze the mixture until the ingredients are mixed. Let it rest for
a few minutes. Form into four small patties and
sauté in a little oil about 5–7 minutes per side.

DILLY DUMPLINGS

¶ serves two as a main meal, four as a side dish
¶ 10–15 minutes

This recipe makes leftover fish into a new filling meal. Cook in Herb Vegetable or Garlic Broth. The dumplings may also be fried as patties.

1 cup cooked flaked leftover fish *or* 1 small can of fish
½ cup raw wheat germ
¼ cup brown rice flour
2 teaspoons dill weed
2 teaspoons oil (optional)
1 teaspoon baking powder
¼ teaspoon salt (optional)

At Home: Place all the dry ingredients in a zip-locking plastic bag. Carry the canned or cooked fish and the oil separately.

In Camp: Flake the leftover fish or drain a can of fish and add to the dry ingredients with the oil and ½ *cup* of water. Drop by the spoonful onto hot broth and cook tightly covered for 10 minutes before checking. The dumplings should be puffed and springy to the touch.

To cook as patties, fry until golden brown on both sides, about 15 minutes.

WHOLE WHEAT AND HERB DUMPLINGS

¶ serves two as a main dish, four as a side dish
¶ 10–15 minutes

Plop these into a soup or broth. Don't peek!

1 cup whole wheat flour
4 tablespoons milk powder
2 tablespoons rolled oats
2 teaspoons baking powder
2 teaspoons dried mixed herbs
2 tablespoons butter

At Home: Combine all the ingredients, rubbing in the butter with your fingertips. Pack in an airtight zip-locking plastic bag.

In Camp: Add ½ *cup* of water to the bagged ingredients and mix. Drop by the spoonful onto bubbling soup or broth. Cover the pot tightly and keep at a steady simmer. Check after 10 minutes. When done, the dumplings are puffed and springy to the touch. Cover and cook for an additional 5 minutes if necessary.

WHOLE WHEAT SPICE DUMPLINGS

¶ 10–15 minutes

Good cooked in Stewed Fruit Soup.

1 cup whole wheat flour
¼ cup chopped nuts
4 tablespoons milk powder
2 tablespoons rolled oats
2 teaspoons baking powder
1 teaspoon mixed spices (cinnamon, nutmeg,
    and so on)
2 tablespoons butter

At Home: Combine all the ingredients, rubbing in the butter with your fingertips. Package in a zip-locking plastic bag.

In Camp: Add ½ *cup* of water to the plastic bag and mix well. Drop the batter by the spoonful onto bubbling soup. Cover tightly and keep at a steady simmer. Check after 10 minutes. The dumplings are puffed and springy to the touch when done. Cook an additional 5 minutes if necessary.

CORN CHEESE DUMPLINGS

¶ serves two as a main dish, four as a side dish
¶ 10–15 minutes

These dumplings are great cooked in Salsa Soup.

½ cup cornmeal
½ cup whole wheat flour
¼ cup milk powder
2 teaspoons baking powder
½ teaspoon cumin
3 tablespoons Parmesan cheese, grated

At Home: Package all the ingredients in a zip-locking plastic bag.

In Camp: Add ½ *cup* of water to the ingredients and mix well. Drop by the spoonful onto bubbling soup or broth. Cover tightly and keep at a steady simmer. Check after 10 minutes. The dumplings should be puffed and springy to the touch. Cook for 5 minutes more if necessary.

BROWN RICE DUMPLINGS

¶ 10–15 minutes

These have a mild, plain flavor. They are good in spicy soups or stews.

¼ cup brown rice flour
¾ cup whole wheat flour
¼ cup raw wheat germ
2 tablespoons milk powder
2 teaspoons baking powder
¼ teaspoon salt
2 tablespoons butter
1 egg (essential)

At Home: Combine all the dry ingredients, and then rub in the butter with your fingertips. Package in a zip-locking plastic bag. Carry the egg separately in an egg container.

In Camp: Add ½ *cup* of water and the egg to the dry ingredients; mix well. Drop by the spoonful onto bubbling soup. Cover and simmer without opening for 10 minutes. The dumplings should be puffed and tender. Cook for 5 minutes more if necessary.

Variations: Add: 1 tablespoon paprika; 1 tablespoon curry powder; 1 tablespoon dried herbs; *or* 1 tablespoon mixed spices (cinnamon, nutmeg, and so on).

ONE-POT LUCK

Simple meals to be made in one pot.
All the ingredients are combined in one
bag, put in a pot of water in camp, and take
15–30 minutes to cook. They are
wholesome, complete meals, satisfying
after a hard day's work.

Sauté any leftovers the next
morning for breakfast or for the next
supper with a sauce or gravy.

CHILI

Put some cheese in your bowl and pour on some of this chili. It's especially good with Cornbread on a cold 10,000-foot night.

1 cup decorticated lentils
¼ cup tomato powder
2 tablespoons masa
1 tablespoon chili powder
1 tablespoon onion flakes *or* 1 fresh onion,
    chopped in camp
1 teaspoon cumin
1 teaspoon oregano
½ teaspoon salt
2 garlic cloves, crushed in camp, *or* ¼ teaspoon
    garlic granules

At Home: Combine the ingredients in a zip-locking plastic bag.

In Camp: Bring *4 cups* of water to a boil and stir in the lentil mixture. Bring back to a boil, cover, reduce the heat, and simmer for 15 minutes. Use a heat diffuser or stir occasionally to prevent sticking if necessary.

LENTIL TOMATO STEW

¶ serves two
¶ 15 minutes

⅔ cup decorticated lentils
½ cup noodles, whole wheat, soyrice, *or* sesame
¼ cup tomato powder
1 tablespoon vegetable bouillon powder *or*
    1 vegetable bouillon cube
2 teaspoons parsley flakes
½ teaspoon salt
¼ teaspoon garlic granules, *or* 2 garlic cloves,
    crushed in camp
dash pepper

At Home: Combine all the ingredients in a zip-locking plastic bag.

In Camp: Bring *5 cups* of water to a boil and stir in the mixture. Return to a boil, cover, reduce heat, and simmer for 15 minutes. Stir occasionally.

LENTILS AND NOODLES

¶ serves two
¶ 15 minutes

¾ cup (decorticated) lentils
½ cup noodles of your choice
2 tablespoons whole wheat flour
2 teaspoons onion flakes *or* 1 fresh onion, minced
    in camp
½ teaspoon salt
⅛ teaspoon cloves, ground
1 bay leaf
dash pepper
1 tablespoon apple cider vinegar, *or* lemon juice

At Home: Combine all the ingredients including the vinegar in an airtight zip-locking plastic bag.

In Camp: Bring *4 cups* of water to a boil and stir in the lentil mixture. Return to a boil, reduce the heat, and simmer covered for 15 minutes. Use a heat diffuser or stir occasionally to prevent sticking if neccessary.

ASIAN RICE AND LENTILS

----------------------------▪▪▪▪▪▪▪▪▪▪▪▪▪▪▪▪

¶ serves two
¶ 20 minutes

Rice and lentils, when eaten together, provide a richer balance of protein than if they are eaten separately.

½ cup basmati rice
½ cup decorticated lentils
2 tablespoons butter
1 fresh onion, chopped in camp, *or* 1 tablespoon
    onion flakes
½ teaspoon salt
½ teaspoon cinnamon
½ teaspoon ginger
½ teaspoon cardamom
2 whole cloves
1 bay leaf
pinch cayenne (optional)

At Home: Combine the ingredients in a zip-locking plastic bag.

In Camp: Bring 2½ *cups* of water to a boil and stir in the mixture. Return to a boil, cover, reduce heat, and simmer 20 minutes. Use a heat diffuser if you have one, or stir occasionally to prevent sticking if necessary.

Variations: Use quinoa (page 184) or precooked brown rice (page 182).

RICE CURRY

Serves two
30 minutes

1 cup basmati rice *or* quinoa
1 fresh onion, chopped in camp, *or* 1 tablespoon
    onion flakes
2 teaspoons curry powder
½ teaspoon salt
handful of each dried fruit: apricots, raisins, dates,
    pears, chopped
handful whole or chopped almonds, cashews,
    or peanuts

At Home: Combine all the ingredients in a zip-locking plastic bag.

In Camp: Bring 3 *cups* of water to a boil and stir in the rice mixture. Return to a boil, cover, reduce the heat, and simmer for 20 minutes. Use a heat diffuser to prevent scorching or stir occasionally to prevent sticking if necessary.

Garnishes: Coconut; salted peanuts.

Variations: Use bulgar: simmer for 5 minutes, remove from the heat, and let stand covered 10 minutes; use millet: toast and crack it at home, simmer for 15 minutes; use precooked brown rice (page 182).

ONE-POT GRAIN AND SEAFOOD

¶ serves two
¶ 15–20 minutes

There are many possibilities for this one-pot meal: using different grains and/or noodles and adding your choice of seasonings and seafood.

1 cup bulgar, basmati rice, millet *or* precooked brown rice *or* noodles
1 tablespoon tomato powder
1 tablespoon celery flakes
1 tablespooon dried bell pepper
1 tablespoon onion flakes *or* 1 fresh onion, chopped in camp
2 garlic cloves, crushed in camp *or* ¼ tablespoon garlic granules *or* ½ tablespoon garlic powder
1 tablespoon of *one* of the following: curry powder; chili powder; mixed herbs; *or* garam masala
4–6 sundried tomatoes, chopped
1 can seafood of your choice
cheese to taste, grated and carried separately

At Home: Mix all the ingredients, except the seafood and the cheese, in a zip-locking plastic bag. (If using precooked brown rice, follow the instructions on page 182).

In Camp: Bring 2½ *cups* of water to a boil and stir in the bulgar mixture. Return to a boil, reduce the heat, and simmer for 5 minutes. Remove from the heat, stir in the seafood and cheese, and let stand 10 minutes. Stir and serve.

If you're using millet, toast and crack it at home. Then increase the cooking time to 15–20 minutes. Serve.

If you're using basmati rice, increase the cooking time to 20 minutes. Serve.

POLENTA CHEESE STEW

½ cup milk powder
½ cup dehydrated corn *or* freeze-dried peas
¼ cup polenta *or* corn grits
1 tablespoon bell pepper flakes
1 bay leaf
1 teaspoon parsley flakes
1 teaspoon onion flakes *or* 1 fresh onion,
    chopped in camp
1 teaspoon celery flakes
2 garlic cloves, crushed in camp, *or* ¼ teaspoon
    garlic granules *or* ¼ teaspoon garlic powder
1 teaspoon savory
½ teaspoon salt
dash cayenne
4–6 sundried tomatoes
¼ cup sunflower seeds (optional)
¼ pound cheddar cheese, chunked in camp, *or*
    1 cup Parmesan, grated

At Home: Combine all the ingredients, except the cheese, in a zip-locking plastic bag. Package the cheese separately.

In Camp: Bring *4 cups* of water to a boil and stir in the polenta mixture. Return to a boil, cover, reduce the heat, and cook for 5–10 minutes. Use a heat diffuser if you have one or stir occasionally to prevent sticking if necessary. Stir in the cheese and serve.

CORN BEAN MUSH

¶ serves two to three
¶ 15–20 minutes

This is a thick mush. It's very good for supper with Garlic Bread or Cheese Toasties.

¾ cup decorticated lentils *or* mung beans
¼ cup dehydrated corn
¼ cup cornmeal
¼ cup soy grits
3 tablespoons tomato powder
1 teaspoon onion flakes *or* 1 fresh onion,
    chopped in camp
1 teaspoon chili powder
1 teaspoon oregano
½ teaspoon salt
2 garlic cloves, crushed in camp, *or* ¼ teaspoon
    garlic granules *or* ½ teaspoon garlic powder
dash cayenne
⅓ cup Parmesan cheese, grated

At Home: Combine all the ingredients, except the cheese, in a zip-locking plastic bag. Package the cheese separately.

In Camp: Bring 4 *cups* of water to a boil and stir in the contents of the bag. Return to a boil, reduce the heat, cover, and simmer for 15 minutes. Use a heat diffuser or stir occasionally to prevent sticking if necessary. Remove from the heat, stir in the cheese, and serve.

SPINACH CHEESE CASSEROLE

- -

¶ serves two
¶ 20 minutes

1¼ cups basmati rice *or* quinoa
½ cup dehydrated spinach flakes
¼ cup dried mushrooms, minced
2 garlic cloves, minced in camp, *or* ¼ teaspoon
    garlic granules
½ teaspoon salt
1 6½-ounce can of shrimp *or* ½ cup freeze-dried
    shrimp
½ pound raw milk cheddar cheese, grated or
    chopped in small chunks, *or* ½ cup Parmesan
    cheese, grated

At Home: Combine all the ingredients, except the cheese and shrimp, in a zip-locking plastic bag. Package the cheese and shrimp separately.

In Camp: Bring 3 *cups* of water to a boil and stir in the rice mixture. Return to a boil, reduce the heat, cover, and simmer for 20 minutes. Use a heat diffuser or stir occasionally to prevent sticking if necessary. Stir in the cheese and shrimp. Heat through and serve. If using freeze-dried shrimp, add them with the rice mixture.

Variations: Use millet, bulgar, or precooked brown rice (page 182).

MUNG BEAN STEW

¶ serves two
¶ 35 minutes

If you haven't ever cooked mung beans as a bean rather than as a sprout, you're in for a delicious surprise. Their flavor somewhat resembles black-eyed peas, and they're good just plain with soy sauce. This recipe makes a very thick souplike broth with the beans for texture and the sesames for crunch.

½ cup mung beans
¼ cup cornmeal
¼ cup sesame seeds, toasted
1 teaspoon onion flakes *or* 1 fresh onion, chopped
    in camp
1 teaspoon parsley flakes
2 garlic cloves, minced in camp, *or* ¼ teaspoon
    garlic granules *or* ½ teaspoon garlic powder
½ teaspoon salt
¼ pound cheddar cheese

At Home: In a frying pan, toast the sesame seeds until they're golden brown. Cool. Then mix all the ingredients, except the cheese, in a zip-locking plastic bag. Package the cheese separately.

In Camp: Bring *3½ cups* of water to a boil and stir in the mung bean mixture. Return to a boil, reduce the heat, cover and simmer for 30 minutes. Use a heat diffuser or stir occasionally to prevent sticking if necessary. Remove from the heat. Cut the cheese into chunks (approximately ½ inch square) and add them to the stew. Cover, let sit for 5 minutes, and serve hot.

CORNMEAL MUNG BEAN STEW

▰▰▰▰▰▰▰▰▰▰▰▰▰▰▰▰▰▰▰▰▰▰▰▰▰▰▰▰▰▰▰▰▰

¶ serves two
¶ 30 minutes

This is a hearty stew, well worth the wait.

½ cup mung beans
½ cup cornmeal, polenta, *or* grits
1 fresh onion, chopped in camp, *or* 1 tablespoon
    onion flakes
1 tablespoon celery flakes
1 tablespoon parsley flakes
2 garlic cloves, crushed in camp, *or* ¼ teaspoon
    garlic granules
1 bay leaf
1 teaspoon cumin
½ teaspoon oregano
½ teaspoon salt
⅛ teaspoon cayenne
1 tablespoon tamari soy sauce

At Home: Mix all the ingredients together in a zip-locking plastic bag.

In Camp: Bring 4 *cups* of water to a boil. Stir in the bean mixture and return to a boil. Reduce the heat, cover, and simmer for 30 minutes. Stir occasionally.

Variations: Add 2 tablespoons tomato powder; stir in grated Parmesan cheese; add a small can of diced green chilis.

MACARONI AND CHEESE

¶ serves two
¶ 10–15 minutes

1 cup macaroni (wheat, *or* buckwheat, *or* soy, etc.)
¼ pound cheese (cheddar, Swiss, jack, *or*
    Parmesan), grated
¼ cup milk powder
1 tablespoon parsley flakes
2 garlic cloves, minced in camp, *or* ¼ teaspoon
    garlic granules *or* ½ teaspoon garlic powder

At Home: Package the cheese, milk powder, garlic,
and parsley in one airtight zip-locking plastic bag
and the macaroni in another.

In Camp: Bring 2–3 *cups* of water to a boil and stir
in the macaroni. Boil 10 minutes. Drain and stir in
the milk and cheese mixture until the cheese is
melted. Serve.

Variations: Add canned tuna or shrimp; add
chopped onion along with the macaroni; add a
little chili powder and ground cumin; use buckwheat noodles and season with oregano; season
with rosemary, basil, or savory; add chopped
walnuts.

GREEN NOODLE SALAD

¶ serves two
¶ 10 minutes

It's a good idea to make this when you have your breakfast fire going; just let it sit in the pot until lunch or supper. It's filling, is very good for supper, especially while you wait for the soup to cook.

8 ounces green *or* mixed-vegetable noodles
¼ cup parsley flakes
1 tablespoon onion flakes
½ teaspoon salt
½ teaspoon basil
¼ teaspoon oregano
¼ teaspoon garlic granules *or* 2 garlic cloves, crushed in camp

At Home: Mix the ingredients together in a zip-locking plastic bag.

In Camp: Bring 2½ *cups* of water to a boil. Stir in the noodle mixture. Boil for 10 minutes. Toss with Miso Dressing or your favorite dressing, and let marinate 1 hour to all day. Toss again before serving.

FRUIT AND NOODLE SALAD

¶ serves two
¶ 5–10 minutes cooking; 1 hour marinating

8 ounces noodle shells or spirals
¾ cup Swiss or Jalsberg cheese, grated, *or* ¼ cup
    Parmesan cheese, grated
⅓ cup mixed dried fruit: such as chopped
    apricots, raisins, currants
⅓ cup nuts, pecans or walnuts (toasted if
    preferred)

DRESSING
¼ cup lemon juice and rind of ½ lemon
½ cup oil
2 teaspoons Dijon mustard
2 cloves garlic, crushed in camp
salt and pepper

At Home: Package the noodles. Combine the nuts
and fruit in a zip-locking plastic bag. Package the
cheese separately. Combine the dressing ingredients in a plastic bottle; put the bottle in a zip-
locking plastic bag to prevent leaks.

In Camp: Boil the noodles for 5–10 minutes or
until barely tender. Drain. Add the fruit mixture
and the dressing. Allow to cool. Add the cheese.
Marinate for 1 hour to all day.

ANCHOVY SPAGHETTI

■■

¶ serves two
¶ 10 minutes

8 ounces spaghetti
1 2-ounce can anchovies in oil
2 large cloves garlic, minced in camp

In Camp: Bring a pot of water to a boil and add the
spaghetti. Boil for 10 minutes and drain. Then
pour the anchovy oil into a pan, add the garlic,
and heat, stirring well until the garlic begins to
sizzle. Mince the anchovies. Add the cooked,
drained spaghetti and the minced anchovies. Toss
to combine, and serve hot or cold.

ALPINE SPAGHETTI

■■

¶ serves two
¶ 10–15 minutes

Pesto!

8 ounces spaghetti or other pasta
1 tablespoon olive oil *or* butter
1 cup Parmesan cheese, grated
3 tablespoons ground dried basil
1 tablespoon parsley flakes
2 garlic cloves, minced in camp, *or* ¼ teaspoon
    garlic granules

At Home: Package the spaghetti in a zip-locking
plastic bag. Carry the olive oil in a plastic lidded
bottle. Combine the remaining ingredients in
another zip-locking plastic bag.

In Camp: Bring a pot of water to a boil and add the
spaghetti. Boil for 10 minutes and drain. Add the
olive oil and toss. Then add the rest of the ingredients and toss again until thoroughly mixed.

SWISS FONDUE

This is a romantic meal for an overnight trip or a cross-country ski lunch.

2 cups (10 ounces) Emmenthal cheese, grated
2 cups (10 ounces) Gruyère cheese, grated
1 tablespoon cornstarch
1 clove garlic
1½ cups dry white wine
3 tablespoons Kirsch
1 teaspoon lemon juice
white pepper, grated nutmeg to taste
French bread for serving

At Home: Grate the cheese and package it. Combine the Kirsch and cornstarch, and package them in a zip-locking plastic bag. Carry a lemon and a bottle of wine. Don't forget the corkscrew!

In Camp: Cut the garlic in half and rub the inside of a cookpot with the cut surface. Use a thick-bottomed pot, or if you're using a thin pot, keep the flame very low or use a heat diffuser. Heat the wine and lemon juice carefully. Add the cheese gradually, stirring continuously in a figure-8 motion. When the mixture is bubbling, add the Kirsch and cornstarch, blended together. Cook 2–3 minutes. Season to taste.

To keep the fondue warm, and not overcooked, place the fondue pot in another pan, with a few inches of water. Place the pans over the cook stove and keep the water at a simmer.

To eat, dip chunks of bread, skewered on a fork or chopstick.

BEER FONDUE

¶ serves three to four
¶ 3–5 minutes

2 cups (8 ounces) cheddar cheese, grated
1 cup beer, preferably ale
1–2 cloves garlic, crushed in camp
2 tablespoons cornstarch
½ teaspoon dry mustard
French bread

At Home: Shred the cheese and package it. Combine the mustard and cornstarch in a zip-locking plastic bag. Carry a can of beer. Carry the garlic separately.

In Camp: Place the beer, cheese, and garlic in a thick-bottomed pan or use a heat diffuser. Cook over low heat, stirring constantly, until the cheese has melted. Blend the cornstarch with a little extra beer or water. Add to the fondue and stir until thickened. (See preceding recipe also.)

Serve with chunks of French bread.

SAUCES

We feel that sauces are a very important part of backpacking food. They turn plain noodles, grains, or patties into something special. Nourishing and inexpensive, they add variety in taste, are simple to make, and are warming on cold days.

TOMATO CURRY SAUCE

¶ serves two
¶ 5–10 minutes

This turns out thick, like a chowder. It's easy and quick to make, even in your tent on a snowy eve. It's good served over noodles or grains.

¼ cup tomato powder
5 teaspoons curry powder
1 tablespoon parsley flakes
½ teaspoon cumin, crushed
½ teaspoon coriander seeds, crushed
½ teaspoon ginger
½ teaspoon salt
½ teaspoon tarragon (optional)
1 fresh onion, chopped in camp, *or* 1 tablespoon
     onion flakes
2 cloves garlic, minced in camp, *or* ¼ teaspoon
     garlic granules *or* ½ teaspoon garlic powder
2 teaspoons tamari soy sauce

At Home: Mix all the ingredients, even the tamari, together in a zip-locking plastic bag.

In Camp: Sauté the chopped onion, if you are using a fresh onion, in a little oil or butter. Add the other ingredients. Stirring constantly, add *2 cups* of water. Bring to a boil, reduce the heat, cover, and simmer for 5–10 minutes.

TOMATO SAUCE

¶ 3½–4 cups
¶ 5 minutes

This is our spaghetti sauce and we also use it over grains and patties. It tastes like fresh homemade sauce.

½ cup tomato powder
¼ cup dried mushrooms, minced
¼ cup dried bell pepper (optional)
3 tablespoons tomato flakes *or* 4–6 sundried tomatoes
1 fresh onion, chopped in camp, *or* 1 tablespoon onion flakes
1 tablespoon parsley flakes
1 tablespoon oregano
1 tablespoon basil
½ teaspoon salt
2 garlic cloves, minced in camp, *or* ¼ teaspoon garlic granules *or* ½ teaspoon garlic powder
1 6½-ounce can crab, clams, or shrimp *or* ½ cup freeze-dried shrimp (optional)

At Home: Combine all the ingredients, except the seafood, in a zip-locking plastic bag.

In Camp: Place the tomato mixture in a cookpot and slowly stir in 3 *cups* of water. Bring to a boil, reduce the heat, cover, and simmer for 5 minutes. Remove from the heat and stir in the seafood.

One-Pot Spaghetti: Add *1 cup* extra water to the sauce and drop in 1 cup of noodles when the sauce comes to a boil.

Variations: Use 1 small can of bonita or mackeral or 1 cup of freshly cooked flaked fish instead of the seafood listed.

CHILI SAUCE

¶ approximately 3½ cups
¶ 5 minutes

Serve this sauce over grains, noodles, polenta, or Journey Cakes.

¼ cup tomato powder
1 small fresh onion, chopped in camp, *or*
    1 tablespoon onion flakes
1 tablespoon whole wheat flour *or* masa *or* corn
    flour
1 teaspoon chili powder
2 teaspoons oregano
1 teaspoon cumin, ground
1 teaspoon parsley flakes
½ teaspoon salt
2 cloves garlic, minced in camp, *or* ¼ teaspoon
    garlic granules *or* ½ teaspoon garlic powder
1 6½-ounce can shrimp *or* ½ cup freeze-dried
    shrimp (optional)

At Home: Mix all the ingredients, except the seafood, in a zip-locking plastic bag.

In Camp: Empty the chili mixture into a cookpot. Slowly stir in 3 *cups* of water. Bring to a boil, reduce the heat, cover, and simmer for 5 minutes. Add the shrimp and heat through. Serve.

SWEET AND SOUR SAUCE

¶ 1 cup
¶ 3–5 minutes

Pour this over noodles or rice, or use it as a sauce with fish.

1 tablespoon dried bell pepper
1 ring dried pineapple, chopped fine
1 tablespoon celery flakes
¼-inch thick slice fresh ginger, chopped fine
1 clove garlic, crushed in camp, *or* ¼ teaspoon
    garlic granules
2–3 tablespoons red wine vinegar
1 teaspoon tamari soy sauce
1 tablespoon honey
1 teaspoon cornstarch

At Home: Package the dried fruit, vegetables, and ginger in a zip-locking plastic bag. In a plastic bottle, combine the honey, vinegar, ginger, tamari, and cornstarch. Place the bottle in a zip-locking plastic bag to avoid spills. Carry garlic along, or add granules to the fruit and vegetable mixture.

In Camp: Empty both packages into a cookpot. Slowly add ¾ *cup* of water. Stirring constantly, bring to a boil, reduce the heat, cover, and simmer for 2–3 minutes.

HOT AND SOUR MISO SAUCE WITH CHINESE MUSHROOMS

❡ 2 cups
❡ 15–30 minutes soaking time; 5 minutes cooking

This sauce adds an Asian flavor to Journey Cakes or patties; or pour it over noodles or rice.

8 Chinese black mushrooms, caps only, finely
    chopped
1 tablespoon toasted sesame seeds
1 tablespoon cornstarch
½ cup miso
1 tablespoon tamari soy sauce
2 tablespoons distilled white vinegar
1–2 tablespoons honey
1 tablespoon toasted sesame oil
3 garlic cloves, crushed in camp, *or* ½ teaspoon
    garlic granules *or* ¾ teaspoon garlic powder
3 25¢-size pieces fresh ginger, chopped
1 small fresh onion, chopped in camp, *or*
    1 tablespoon dried onion (optional)
1 tablespoon chili paste *or* ½–1 tablespoon dried
    red chili flakes (optional)

At Home: Package the mushrooms and sesame seeds in two separate zip-locking plastic bags. Combine the remaining ingredients in a plastic bottle. Place the bottle in a zip-locking plastic bag to prevent spills. If you are using a fresh onion, carry it along whole and chop it in camp.

In Camp: Soak the mushrooms in ½ *cup* of water for 15–30 minutes. Pour the miso mixture into a cookpot and slowly add 1¼ *cups* of water and the soaking liquid. Stirring constantly, bring to a boil, cover, reduce the heat, and simmer for 3–5 minutes. Then add the toasted sesame seeds.

TAHINI ORANGE SAUCE

¶ approximately 2 cups
¶ 5 minutes

This sauce has the flavor of country gravy. Serve it over whole-grain pastas, carrot cakes, patties, or cooked potatoes.

½ cup sesame tahini
2 tablespoons whole wheat flour
1 tablespoon tamari soy sauce
1 teaspoon orange rind, grated
1 teaspoon honey
1 garlic clove, crushed in camp

At Home: Mix all the ingredients together in a zip-locking plastic bag.

In Camp: Put the tahini mixture in a cookpot and place over moderate heat. Slowly stir in *1¼ cups* of water and bring to a boil, stirring constantly. Reduce the heat, cover, and simmer for 2–3 minutes.

TOASTED CASHEW GINGER SAUCE

¶ 2 cups
¶ 5 minutes

This has a sweet, toasted cashew flavor. Serve it over noodles, grains, or Journey Cakes. Save leftovers as a spread.

1 cup raw cashews
¼ cup milk powder
2 teaspoons cornstarch
1–2 teaspoons fresh ginger root, grated
1 teaspoon tamari soy sauce

At Home: Roast the cashews in a moderate (350°) oven for 8 minutes or stir in a frying pan until golden brown. Then cool and grind them. Combine the nuts with the remaining ingredients in a zip-locking plastic bag.

In Camp: Place the mixture in a cookpot and gradually stir in 1½ *cups* of water. Use moderate heat to bring the mixture to a boil, stirring constantly. Reduce the heat, cover, and simmer for 2–3 minutes.

TAHINI DIPPING SAUCE

¶ makes ½ cup

This is great over Falafel or as a sauce for Journey Cakes.

¼ cup sesame tahini
4 tablespoons lemon juice
3 garlic cloves, crushed or minced fine in camp
1 teaspoon cilantro
pinch salt
3–4 tablespoons water

At Home: Combine all ingredients and mix well. Package in a lidded plastic bottle.

In Camp: Serve with Falafel, fresh vegetables, or Journey Cakes.

MISO MUSTARD SAUCE

¶ 1½ cups
¶ 3–5 minutes

This is a hearty sauce, good over Journey Cakes.

2 tablespoons whole wheat flour
1 tablespoon miso
1 tablespoon mustard (Dijon style)
1 garlic clove, crushed in camp, *or* ⅛ teaspoon
     garlic granules *or* ¼ teaspoon garlic powder
¼ teaspoon orange peel
dash of honey

At Home: Combine all the ingredients in a lidded plastic container.

In Camp: Put the miso mixture into a cookpot and gradually stir in *1 cup* of water. Place over moderate heat and bring to a boil. Reduce the heat, cover, and simmer for 2–3 minutes.

Variations: Use ginger instead of orange peel; make a horseradish sauce by replacing the mustard with 1 tablespoon of horseradish powder (wasabi).

NUT BUTTER SAUCE

¶ approximately 1½ cups
¶ 3–5 minutes

½ cup nut butter
1 tablespoon whole wheat flour
pinch garlic granules
dash cayenne
1 teaspoon tamari soy sauce

At Home: Combine all the ingredients in a zip-locking plastic bag.

In Camp: Place the nut butter mixture in a cookpot and stir in *1 cup* of water. Bring to a boil, reduce the heat, cover, and simmer for 3–5 minutes.

BASIC WHITE SAUCE

¶ 1 cup
¶ 3–5 minutes

2 tablespoons flour
½ cup milk powder
½ teaspoon dry mustard
salt, pepper, nutmeg to taste

At Home: Mix all the ingredients together in a zip-locking plastic bag.

In Camp: Place the mixture in a cookpot and slowly stir in *1 cup* of water. Over moderate heat, stir until the sauce boils and thickens. Cover and simmer for 3–5 minutes to cook the flour.

Variations: To make a *cheese sauce*—add ½–1 cup grated cheddar cheese *or* ½ cup grated Parmesan. To make a *clam sauce* for pasta—add 2 crushed garlic cloves, 1 tablespoon dried basil, 1 table-spoon dried oregano, a can of clams and their juice. To make a *curry sauce*—add 1–2 tablespoons curry powder, a handful of raisins.

CHEESE SAUCE

¶ approximately 2 cups
¶ 5 minutes

This is a very quick, very creamy sauce.

½ cup milk powder
2 tablespoons whole wheat flour
1 garlic clove, minced in camp, *or* ⅛ teaspoon
     garlic granules *or* ¼ teaspoon garlic powder
1 teaspoon parsley flakes
½ teaspoon dry mustard
dash cayenne
¼ pound grated Monterey jack *or* Parmesan
     cheese

At Home: Combine all the ingredients, except the
cheese, in a zip-locking plastic bag. Carry the
cheese well sealed in another zip-locking
plastic bag.

In Camp: Place the mixture in a cookpot and
slowly stir in 1¾ *cups* of water. Over moderate
heat, bring to a boil, stirring constantly. Cover,
reduce the heat, and simmer 2–3 minutes. Stir in
the cheese.

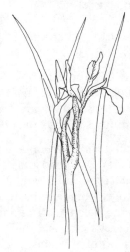

TUNA SAUCE

¶ approximately 2½ cups
¶ 3–5 minutes

This recipe is for one of those nights when you counted on fresh fish all day, but for some reason they just weren't biting.

1 6½-ounce can albacore tuna in oil
¼ cup milk powder
2 tablespoons whole wheat flour
1 tablespoon parsley flakes
1 garlic clove, minced in camp, *or* ¼ teaspoon
    garlic powder *or* ⅛ teaspoon garlic granules
½ teaspoon dill weed
dash cayenne *or* black pepper

At Home: Combine all the ingredients, except the tuna, in a zip-locking plastic bag.

In Camp: Combine all ingredients, including the tuna with its oil, in a cookpot and stir in *1 cup* of water. Bring to a boil over moderate heat and then simmer for 2–3 minutes to cook the flour. Serve hot over grains, noodles, patties, or even broken pieces of bread or toast.

This recipe can serve four with one can of tuna by doubling everything else.

MUSHROOM SAUCE

¶ 1 cup
¶ 3–5 minutes cooking; 5 minutes standing

This is a thick, rich sauce, with a mushroom flavor.

⅓ cup dried mushrooms, minced
2 tablespoons whole wheat flour
2 tablespoons milk powder
1 tablespoon dried chopped chives
2 teaspoons vegetable bouillon powder *or*
    1 vegetable bouillon cube
1 teaspoon parsley flakes
1 garlic clove, minced in camp, *or* ⅛ teaspoon
    garlic granules
dash pepper

At Home: Combine all the ingredients in a zip-locking plastic bag.

In Camp: Place the mushroom mixture in a cook-pot. Slowly stir in *1¼ cups* of water. Bring to a boil, reduce the heat, cover, and simmer for 3–5 minutes. Remove from the heat. Let the sauce stand for 5 minutes.

GARLIC SAUCE

¶ 1½ cups
¶ 5 minutes

This should be made with fresh garlic.

3–4 garlic cloves, crushed
2 tablespoons whole wheat flour
1 tablespoon vegetable bouillon powder *or*
    1 vegetable bouillon cube
¼ teaspoon black pepper
pinch cayenne

At Home: Combine all the ingredients a zip-locking plastic bag.

In Camp: Place the garlic mixture in a cookpot. Slowly stir in *1 cup* of water. Bring to a boil, stirring constantly. Reduce the heat, cover, and simmer for 3–5 minutes.

CURRY SAUCE

¶ 1 cup
¶ 3–5 minutes

2 tablespoons milk powder
2 tablespoons whole wheat flour
1 teaspoon onion flakes
1 garlic clove, minced in camp, *or* ⅛ teaspoon
    garlic granules *or* ¼ teaspoon garlic powder
1 teaspoon parsley flakes
1 teaspoon curry powder
¼ teaspoon salt

At Home: Combine all the ingredients in an airtight plastic bag.

In Camp: Empty the bag into a cookpot. Slowly stir in *1 cup* of water. Bring to a boil, reduce the heat, cover, and simmer for 2–3 minutes.

CASHEW SAUCE

¶ approximately 3 cups
¶ 5 minutes

This is a mild sauce. It's simple to make and adds protein to the meal.

¾ cup raw cashews, ground fine
2 tablespoons arrowroot powder *or* cornstarch
1 teaspoon parsley flakes
1 teaspoon onion powder *or* flakes
½ teaspoon celery flakes
⅛ teaspoon celery seeds
1 teaspoon tamari soy sauce

At Home: Grind the cashews in a blender, coffee grinder, or electric mill. Then combine all ingredients in a zip-locking plastic bag.

In Camp: Put the mixture in a cookpot. Slowly stir in 2½–3 *cups* of water and stir over medium heat until thick. Serve hot.

SEAFOOD

Salmon in Tomato Orange Sauce,
Crab a la King,
Shrimp Curry
Baked Trout

SALMON IN TOMATO ORANGE SAUCE

¶ serves four
¶ 5 minutes

Surprise your friends in the backcountry with this delightful meal. Serve over pasta, rice, or steamed Cornbread. Serves two as a chowder with Singing Hinnies.

¼ cup tomato powder
3 tablespoons whole wheat flour
1 fresh onion, chopped in camp, *or* 1 tablespoon
    onion flakes
⅓ cup dried mushrooms, chopped fine
2 garlic cloves, crushed in camp, *or* ¼ teaspoon
    garlic granules *or* ½ teaspoon garlic powder
1 teaspoon orange rind, fresh *or* dried, grated
½ teaspoon salt
4–6 sundried tomatoes, chopped
pinch cayenne
1 can salmon

At Home: Package all the ingredients, except the salmon, in a zip-locking plastic bag. If you are using a fresh onion, carry it whole.

In Camp: Place the ingredients in a cookpot and stir in 2½ *cups* of water. If you are using a fresh onion, chop and add it. Bring the mixture to a boil over moderate heat, stirring constantly. Reduce the heat, cover, and simmer for 2–3 minutes.

Variations: Replace the salmon with any desired seafood.

SHRIMP CURRY

Serve with a hot bread.

¼ cup tomato powder
5 teaspoons curry powder
1 tablespoon parsley flakes
½ teaspoon cumin seeds, crushed
½ teaspoon coriander seeds, crushed
½ teaspoon ginger
½ teaspoon tarragon (optional)
1 fresh onion, chopped in camp, *or* 1 tablespoon
    onion flakes
2 garlic cloves, minced in camp, *or* ¼ teaspoon
    garlic granules *or* ½ teaspoon garlic powder
2 teaspoons tamari soy sauce
1 6½-ounce can shrimp

At Home: Combine all the ingredients, except the shrimp, in an airtight zip-locking plastic bag.

In Camp: Sauté the chopped onion in oil if you are using fresh onion, and stir in the rest of the mixture. Quickly stir in 2 *cups* of water and bring to a boil. Reduce the heat, cover, and simmer for 5–10 minutes. Add the shrimp, heat through, and serve.

Variations: Add any seafood of your choice.

CRAB A LA KING

Here you have the luxury of crab in a complete meal!

½ cup Parmesan cheese, grated
½ cup milk powder
4 tablespoons whole wheat flour
2 tablespoons dried chives
1½ tablespoons dried bell pepper
2 garlic cloves, minced in camp
¼ teaspoon nutmeg
pinch cayenne
6–8 sundried tomatoes, chopped
1 6½-ounce can crab
1 cup spinach egg noodles

At Home: Combine the ingredients, except the crab and noodles, and package in a zip-locking plastic bag. Package the noodles and crab separately.

In Camp: Cook the noodles in boiling water, for about 7–10 minutes, drain, and set aside. Empty the contents of the bag into the cookpot and gradually stir in 2 *cups* of water. Over a moderate heat, stirring constantly, bring to a boil. Reduce the heat, cover, and simmer 3–5 minutes. Stir in the crab and noodles, heat through, and serve.

BAKED TROUT

¶ serves two
¶ 20–30 minutes

This is a good recipe for one of the first nights out, when you still might have a baked potato left, and the fishing has been fine.

4 medium-sized trout, or enough fish for
    two people
1 baked potato, cubed in camp
½ teaspoon thyme
salt and pepper to taste
butter
foil

At Home: Carry the spices premixed, or use spices from your camp kitchen.

In Camp: Lay out two generous pieces of foil. Place the clean fish, enough for one serving, in each piece of foil. Season well with salt, pepper, and thyme. Scatter the potato around the fish, and dot with butter. Seal the foil with the seams to the top. In a frying pan, place about ½ *inch* of water. Bring to a simmer. Place in the foil packages, put the lid on, and cook at a simmer for 20–30 minutes. The time depends on the thickness of the fish.

Eat right from the package.

BAKED TROUT WITH GRAIN STUFFING

¶ serves two
¶ 20–30 minutes

enough fresh trout for two
½ cup instant wild rice *or* bulgar
1 lemon, sliced
1 fresh onion, chopped in camp
2 garlic cloves, crushed in camp
1 tablespoon parsley flakes
1 teaspoon dill
salt to taste
1–2 tablespoons butter
foil

At Home: Package the seasonings together. Package the rice or bulgar separately.

In Camp: Bring *1 cup* of water to a boil, add the rice or bulgar, cover, and set aside to soak for 15 minutes. Drain off any excess water, add the seasonings and butter, and stir to mix.

Place the fish on two generous pieces of foil. Stuff the cavity of each fish with the grain mixture. Scatter any extra around the fish. Dot the fish with butter and top with slices of lemon. Seal the foil with the seams to the top. In a frying pan, bring ½ *inch* of water to a simmer. Add the foil packages, cover, and simmer for 20–30 minutes or until the fish is tender. This depends on the thickness of the fish.

Eat right from the package.

BASIC FRIED TROUT

We always carry a bag of breading mixture for frying trout. Here are a few combinations that we
enjoy:

cornmeal; salt, pepper, sage (optional) to taste
1 part cornmeal, 1 part corn flour; salt, pepper
      to taste
whole wheat flour; salt, pepper to taste
whole wheat flour; salt, pepper, garlic granules,
      sesame seeds to taste

Clean freshly caught fish and, while still wet, roll
in mixture and fry. Fish will be done when the
flesh is no longer translucent and flakes away
when pried with a fork. (The time depends on the
thickness of the fish.) Sprinkle on a little lemon
juice, if you like.

BEN'S FRIED TROUT

Wash and clean fresh-caught trout, leaving it a little moist. Sprinkle a combination of garlic granules, salt, and pepper on one side, and put that side down in a hot frying pan with a little oil. While cooking, sprinkle more of the same on the other side. Turn, and fry until done.

IRIKI

If you get a chance to go to Chinatown, or to a place where they carry Chinese or Japanese products, you might see these very small dried fish, about 2 inches long. These are very lightweight and a real treat for a snack. They are very high in protein, as the whole fish is eaten, bones and all.

Oil the bottom of frying pan, and put in a handful of the dried fish. Brown until toasty and crunchy, sprinkle with soy sauce, and stir in a little bit more. Remove from pan and cool on a plate.

GRAINS

Here are a few grain recipes that are good with sauces or gravies poured over them or as a complement to freshly caught fish.

PLAIN BROWN RICE

Brown rice cooked in camp over a fuel stove is not very practical, as at high elevations it will take over an hour to cook. But it is possible to have this tasty grain by either pressure cooking (see page 23) or by cooking the rice at home.

1 cup brown rice (we prefer short grain)
pinch salt
2½ cups water
butter

At Home: Bring the ingredients to a simmer, cover, and simmer for about 45 minutes or until the grains are tender. Don't stir the rice until it is cooked.

Wait until the rice is cold, then package it in serving-size portions (¾–1 cup), in airtight zip-locking plastic bags. Add about 1 tablespoon of butter to each portion—bury the butter in the rice. The rice will stay fresh for 2–3 days. If the rice gets sour, rinse it in cold water and drain.

Variations: Add 1–2 tablespoons of dried herbs.

BASMATI RICE

This whole-grain white rice comes from Pakistan. The air is perfumed by it.

In Camp: Cook ½ cup of rice per person in twice as much water as rice. Add a pinch of salt and a tablespoon of butter. Cover. Simmer for 20–25 minutes. Fluff with a fork.

Serve with a sauce or as a substitute for any grain.

Variations: Add 1 tablespoon dried mixed herbs; add 2 teaspoons curry powder.

INSTANT WILD RICE

¶ serves two
¶ 7–10 minutes

This is a new item on the market. The rice is pre-cooked and then dried. It takes 7 minutes to soak in boiled water. Here is a recipe for buttered wild rice with a few variations. For mail order information, turn to Food Sources, page 245.

1 4-ounce package instant wild rice (approximately 1½ cups)
2–3 tablespoons butter

In Camp: Bring 2 *cups* of water to a boil in a cookpot. Stir in the rice, remove from the heat, and let soak for approximately 7 minutes. Drain the excess liquid. In a pan, melt the butter and stir in the soaked rice. Sauté 2–3 minutes. Serve.

Variations: Sauté 1–2 crushed garlic cloves in the butter first; add 1 tablespoon mixed dried herbs; serve with a sauce or gravy; use it to stuff fresh fish to be steamed; add a handful of nuts and raisins.

QUINOA

¶ 10–15 minutes

Pronounced keenwa, this is a recently rediscovered grain that comes from the Andean Mountain regions of South America. Quinoa was a staple
food of the Inca civilization and is still known as
the Mother Grain. It contains more protein than
any other grain, is a complete protein by itself,
and is also high in fiber, minerals, and vitamins.
Its high nutritional value and its quick and easy
preparation make it a perfect food for backpacking
and camping. It can replace any grain in any
recipe; just remember to shorten the cooking time
to 15 minutes.

For distribution nearest you, write the Quinoa
Corp., address on page 245.

Basic Quinoa:
1 cup quinoa

In Camp: Rinse quinoa in cold water and drain.
Place it in a cookpot with *2 cups* of water and bring
to a boil. Reduce the heat, cover, and cook for 10–
15 minutes or until all the water is absorbed. Use a
heat diffuser or stir occasionally to prevent sticking if necessary. The grains will turn from white to
transparent.

MOROCCAN COUSCOUS

¶ serves two
¶ 3–5 minutes

This is a great dish or, for a complete meal, serve it with cheese and pocket bread.

1 cup couscous
2 tablespoons dried chives
2 teaspoons curry powder
1 vegetable bouillon cube *or* 1 tablespoon
    vegetable bouillon powder
3 garlic cloves, minced in camp, *or* ½ teaspoon
    garlic granules *or* ¾ teaspoon garlic powder
6–8 sundried tomatoes, diced
handful of pistachios *or* pine nuts (optional)

At Home: Combine all the ingredients in a zip-locking plastic bag.

In Camp: Empty the contents of the bag into a cookpot. Stir in *2 cups* of water. Over moderate heat with the cover on, bring to a boil and cook 1–2 minutes. Turn off the heat and let the couscous sit undisturbed 3–5 minutes. Fluff with a fork. Serve.

TABOULI

This may be made in the morning and left to cool in the shade until lunch or dinner. Toss and serve with Falafel, pocket bread, or Tahini Dipping Sauce.

1 cup bulgar
1 fresh onion, chopped fine, *or* 1 tablespoon onion
    flakes
¼ cup parsley flakes
1 tablespoon dried mint
black pepper and salt to taste
4–6 sundried tomatoes
½ cup oil
½ cup lemon juice

At Home: Mix all the dry ingredients in a zip-locking plastic bag. If you are using a fresh onion, carry it whole and chop it in camp. Carry the oil and lemon juice together in a plastic bottle. Put the bottle in a zip-locking plastic bag to prevent leaks.

In Camp: Bring 2 *cups* of water to a boil. Stir in the bulgar mixture, cover the pot, and remove from the heat. Let the pot stand for 10 minutes. Toss in the oil and lemon juice. Let the mixture stand until cool. Toss again and serve.

SPANISH BULGAR

¶ serves two
¶ 5 minutes cooking;
10 minutes standing

This takes only minutes to cook—and is a great grain dish. Serve it with Fish Patties or melt in some cheese.

1 cup bulgar
¼ cup mushrooms, dried and chopped
1 tablespoon tomato powder
1 tablespoon celery flakes
1 tablespoon onion flakes *or* 1 fresh onion,
    chopped in camp
1 tablespoon dried bell pepper
2 garlic cloves, minced in camp, *or* ¼ teaspoon
    garlic granules *or* ½ teaspoon garlic powder
1 teaspoon cumin powder
½ teaspoon red chilis, powdered
pinch salt

At Home: Mix all the ingredients in a zip-locking plastic bag. If you are using a fresh onion, carry it whole and chop it in camp.

In Camp: Bring 2½ *cups* of water to a boil. Stir in the bulgar mixture, cover, reduce the heat, and simmer for 2–5 minutes. Remove from the heat and let stand for 5–10 minutes. Serve.

MUSHROOM BULGAR

¶ serves two
¶ 5 minutes cooking; 10 minutes standing

1 cup bulgar
¼ cup dried mushrooms, chopped
3 tablespoons sesame seeds, toasted
1 tablespoon dried onion flakes *or* 1 fresh onion,
    chopped in camp
1 vegetable bouillon cube *or* 1 tablespoon
    vegetable bouillon powder
1 tablespoon celery flakes
1 tablespoon parsley flakes
1 teaspoon dried savory

At Home: Mix the ingredients together in a zip-locking plastic bag. If you are using a fresh onion, carry it separately.

In Camp: Place the ingredients in a cookpot (add the chopped fresh onion if you are using a fresh onion), and add 2–2½ *cups* of water. Bring to a boil, cover the pot, reduce the heat, and simmer for 5 minutes. Remove from the heat, but leave the lid on. Set aside for 10 minutes to complete the cooking. Serve.

BULGAR WITH SAGE

¶ serves two
¶ 5 minutes cooking; 10 minutes standing

1 cup bulgar
2 tablespoons celery flakes
1 tablespoon onion flakes, *or* 1 fresh onion,
      chopped in camp
2 garlic cloves, crushed in camp, *or* ¼ teaspoon
      garlic granules *or* ½ teaspoon garlic powder
½ teaspoon each sage and thyme
salt to taste
2 tablespoons peanut butter or any roasted
      nut butter

At Home: Mix all the ingredients, except the peanut butter, in a zip-locking plastic bag. Package
the peanut butter in a squeeze tube or a wide-
mouth plastic bottle with a lid. Carry the fresh
onion separately.

In Camp: Bring 2 *cups* of water to a boil. Stir in the
bulgar mixture. Return to a boil, reduce the heat,
cover, and simmer for 5 minutes. Remove from
the heat, stir in the peanut butter, and let stand,
covered, for 10 minutes. Serve.

MILLET PILAF

¶ serves two
¶ 15–20 minutes

Pour Curry Sauce or Nut Butter Gravy over this
for a great meal.

1 cup millet
3 tablespoons butter
2 tablespoons raisins
2-inch piece cinnamon stick
5 cloves, whole
1 fresh onion, chopped in camp
1 fresh carrot, chopped in camp

At Home: In a frying pan, over moderate heat, toast
the millet to a golden brown, stirring frequently.
Cool. Then crack it in a blender. Combine the
cracked millet with butter, raisins, cinnamon, and
cloves in a zip-locking plastic bag. Carry the carrot
and onion in another zip-locking bag.

In Camp: Chop the onion and carrot. Bring 2½
cups of water to a boil. Stir in the millet mixture
and chopped vegetables. Return to a boil, reduce
the heat, cover the pot, and simmer for 15–20
minutes. Use a heat diffuser or stir occasionally to
prevent sticking if necessary.

BUCKWHEAT STRING BEANS

If you get this going and then fry some trout, both will probably be done at the same time, offering a satisfying, complete meal.

1 cup toasted buckwheat groats
¾ cup dehydrated *or* ⅓ cup freeze-dried
    string beans
½ cup dried mushrooms, minced
1 tablespoon onion flakes *or* fresh onion, chopped
    in camp
2 garlic cloves, crushed in camp, *or* ¼ teaspoon
    garlic granules *or* ½ teaspoon garlic powder
1 teaspoon oregano

At Home: Combine all the ingredients in a zip-locking plastic bag. If you're using a fresh onion, carry it separately.

In Camp: Bring 3 ¾ *cups* of water to a boil; stir in the buckwheat mixture and return to a boil. Reduce the heat, cover, and simmer for 20 minutes. Use a heat diffuser or stir occasionally to prevent sticking if necessary. Serve with tamari soy sauce or Sesame Salt.

Variations: Make this a one-pot meal by adding a handful of dried shrimp at the beginning or a small can of shrimp at the end.

GRAB BAG

This section suggests an alternative way of packaging food for cooking along the trail, allowing you to plan your menu as you go. With a few basic ingredients you can create a variety of meals without repetition. For instance, a combination of rolled oats and wheat mixed with raisins, nuts, and cinnamon can be a cereal served for breakfast, and when mixed with tomato powder, herbs, fresh onion, and garlic it's a one-pot meal.

To carry your food this way, package the staples for each basic recipe in zip-locking plastic bags, leaving the dried fruits, vegetables, nuts, herbs, spices, and so forth to go in separate small plastic bottles or bags.

Use your imagination!

POLENTA MUSH

¶ serves two
¶ 5–10 minutes

Polenta is a special grind of corn that can be found in natural food stores or in any market that sells Italian food. If you can't find polenta, substitute an equal amount of corn grits. Polenta cooks into a thick mush and can be sweet or savory depending on what you add. When cooled, the mush can be sliced, sautéd, and served with a sauce. The basic recipe is for two servings. Halve, double, triple, etc., the recipe according to your needs.

Basic Recipe:

1 cup polenta or corn grits
2 tablespoons soy grits
½ teaspoon salt

At Home: Package all the ingredients in a zip-locking plastic bag.

In Camp: Bring *4 cups* of water to a boil. Stir in the polenta mixture, return to a boil, cover the pan, and reduce the heat to low. Use a heat diffuser if necessary to prevent scorching. Cook 5–10 minutes without stirring.

Variations:

Cereal: Prepare the basic recipe. Then stir in and heat through any of the following to taste: dried fruit, nuts, seeds, milk powder, cinnamon, honey, butter, maple syrup.

One-Pot Meal: Bring *4 cups* of water to a boil. Stir in the basic recipe and any one of the following combinations. Return to a boil, cover the pot, reduce the heat to low, and cook for 5–10 minutes. Use a heat diffuser if necessary to avoid scorching. If using cheese or seafood, stir it in just before serving.
½ cup walnuts or pecans, ¼ pound cheddar

cheese, cubed, and fresh garlic and onions
  to taste
chili powder, cumin, oregano, onions, and garlic
  to taste, and jack cheese
a can of albacore, and dill to taste

Polenta Mush Cakes: Prepare the basic recipe and
allow it to cool. Slice it or form into patties, and
sauté in a little butter or oil. Serve with maple
syrup or honey.

MOUNTAIN GRUEL

¶ serves two
¶ 5–10 minutes

This is a basic recipe with many options: soup,
cereal, one-pot meal, or pudding.

Basic Recipe:
½ cup rolled oats
½ cup rolled wheat
2 tablespoons soy grits
½ teaspoon salt

At Home: Combine all the ingredients in a zip-
locking plastic bag.

In Camp: Combine the oat mixture with 2 *cups* of
water and bring to a boil over moderate heat, stirring occasionally. Reduce the heat and cook slowly
for 5–10 minutes.

Variations:
Cereal: Just before serving, stir in any combination
of: raisins or other dried fruit, nuts or seeds, raw
wheat germ, milk powder, cinnamon, honey,
maple syrup.

Toasted Cereal: Before adding the water to the basic
recipe, toast grains first by stirring constantly in

any unoiled pan over moderate heat. The grains will have a toasted aroma. Then proceed as in the basic recipe. Garnish with: Sesame Salt, soy sauce, nuts or seeds.

Soup: Prepare the basic recipe but add *4 cups* of water instead of 2. Along with the water add any one of the following combinations to taste:

tomato powder, miso, cumin, and oregano

vegetable bouillon cube, onion, and garlic

Parmesan cheese, milk powder, garlic, and basil

Dessert: Prepare the basic recipe and add any combination of the following to taste: vanilla, milk powder, allspice, cloves, nutmeg, and/or ginger, molasses *or* honey *or* maple syrup, Home-Dried Apples.

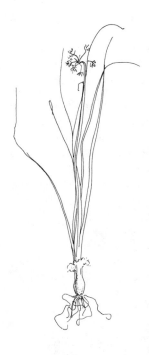

DOUG'S BULGAR

¶ serves two
¶ 15–20 minutes

Bulgar is precooked cracked wheat, which makes it a quick-cooking dinner base, especially for building seafood variations.

Basic recipe:
1 cup bulgar
2 tablespoons soy grits
1 tablespoon vegetable bouillon powder *or*
      1 vegetable bouillon cube
2 garlic cloves, crushed in camp, *or* ¼ teaspoon
      garlic granules *or* ½ teaspoon garlic powder
1–2 bay leaves

At Home: Combine all the ingredients in a zip-locking plastic bag.

In Camp: Bring *2–4 cups* of water (depending on thickness desired) to a boil. Stir in the bulgar mixture and return to a boil. Cover the pan and reduce the heat to low. Use a heat diffuser to prevent scorching if necessary. Cook 10–15 minutes.

Variations: Add small handfuls of your favorite dried vegetables; add a chopped fresh onion and/or carrot; add your favorite mixed herbs or soy sauce. Just before serving, stir in canned albacore, salmon, mackerel, shrimp, or crab.

DESSERTS

For children and celebrations. Make a
surprise birthday cake, snow ice cream, or a
sweet after a light supper.

HIGH MOUNTAIN PIE

¶ serves two
¶ 40 minutes

This is a favorite of ours. It may be baked as a cake or served like shortcake.

Group 1:
2 cups mixed dried fruit: apricots, apples, figs,
    prunes, raisins, pears, pineapple, dates
large handful of walnuts *or* pecans
1 tablespoon honey
1 teaspoon cinnamon

Group 2:
1 cup brown rice flour
¼ cup raw wheat germ
2 tablespoons milk powder
1 teaspoon baking powder
½ teaspoon cinnamon
½ teaspoon salt
¼ teaspoon nutmeg
2 tablespoons honey
2 tablespoons butter

At Home: Combine group 1 in a zip-locking plastic bag. Combine group 2 and rub in the butter with your fingertips. Also package in a zip-locking plastic bag.

In Camp: Place the dried fruit mixture in a frying pan with enough water to cover the fruit. Cook, covered, over low heat for 10 minutes. Stir occasionally and add more water as necessary.

Add ½ *cup* of water to the rice flour mixture and stir to combine. Remove the fruit mixture from the heat, and pour batter over it. Cover the pan tightly with aluminum foil, crimping it over the pan edges. Place the pan over low heat. (It is a good idea to use a heat diffuser between the pan and the stove.) Bake for 30 minutes. The crust will be springy to the touch. Serve warm.

Variations: Cook the fruit as above. Make the batter thinner and cook it in a frying pan as pancakes. Pour the fruit over the cakes and serve hot.

APPLE SAUCE

¶ serves two
¶ 10 minutes

2 cups Home-Dried Apples, chopped and pressed
    gently down into measuring cup
water
1 tablespoon honey

In Camp: Add enough water to just barely cover the apples in a cookpot. Simmer until the apples are soft and saucy. Add the honey. Serve warm or cold.

Variations: Add ½ teaspoon cinnamon; a squeeze of lemon; raisins; nuts.

APPLE CRISP

This is surprisingly delicious and easy to make.
Everybody loves it.

¼ pound Home-Dried Apples
½ teaspoon cinnamon
big pinch nutmeg
squeeze lemon
1 cup rolled oats
¼ cup whole wheat flour
2 tablespoons butter
2 teaspoons honey
¼ teaspoon salt
1 teaspoon mixed spices (optional)

At Home: Combine the apples, cinnamon, and
nutmeg, and squeeze in some lemon juice. Package in a zip-locking plastic bag. Combine the
remaining ingredients in another zip-locking
plastic bag.

In Camp: Soak the apple mixture in *1½–2 cups* of
water for 10 minutes. When soaked, turn the mixture into a cookpot. Sprinkle on the oat mixture
and cover the pan. Place over low heat. Use a heat
diffuser to prevent scorching and cook for 15–20
minutes.

APPLE BARLEY PUDDING

¶ serves four
¶ 10–15 minutes

This is a good dessert after a light supper.

1 cup rolled oats *or* barley
1 cup Home-Dried Apples, chopped
½ cup raisins
handful nuts
1 teaspoon cinnamon
½ teaspoon nutmeg
dash cloves (optional)
honey to taste

At Home: Combine the ingredients in a zip-locking plastic bag.

In Camp: Place the mixture in a cookpot and add *3 cups* of water. Bring to a boil over moderate heat, cover, and reduce the heat to low. Simmer 5–10 minutes. Serve hot.

TAPIOCA FRUIT PUDDING

¶ serves two
¶ 5–10 minutes cooking

This is a bit like Stewed Fruit, but with a texture and flavor all its own.

2 cups dried fruit and nuts, chopped
3 tablespoons tapioca
1 tablespoon rose hip powder
1 tablespoon honey
juice of 1 lemon *or* lime

At Home: Combine the ingredients in a zip-locking plastic bag.

In Camp: Place the fruit mixture in a cookpot and stir in 2½ *cups* of water. Let the mixture stand for 5 minutes–1 hour. Then bring it to a boil, stirring constantly. Cook 5–10 minutes. Let the pudding stand to cool or serve warm.

CREAMY TAPIOCA PUDDING

¶ serves two
¶ 5–10 minutes cooking

⅔ cup milk powder
3 tablespoons tapioca
1 tablespoon honey
1 teaspoon vanilla
pinch salt

At Home: Combine all the ingredients in a zip-locking plastic bag.

In Camp: Place the tapioca mixture in a cookpot. Slowly stir in 2 *cups* of water, and let the mixture sit for 5 minutes. Then bring it to a boil, stirring constantly. Remove the pot from the heat. Serve the pudding warm or let it stand to cool.

Variation: For carob pudding, add 2 tablespoons of carob powder.

CUP OF CUSTARD

¶ serves two to four
¶ 3 minutes

This dessert brings back memories of childhood. Add fruit, nuts, or coconut for four servings, or pour it over Golden Delights.

½ cup milk powder
1 tablespoon cornstarch
1–2 tablespoons date sugar *or* honey
1 teaspoon vanilla (optional)

At Home: Combine the ingredients in a zip-locking plastic bag. If you are using vanilla, stir it into the honey or date sugar before adding these ingredients to the plastic bag.

In Camp: Put the contents of the package into a cookpot. Slowly add *1 cup* of water, stirring constantly. Over low heat, still stirring, bring to a simmer. Simmer for 2–3 minutes to cook the cornstarch. Serve warm or cold.

Variation: Add 2 tablespoons of cocoa for a chocolate custard.

GOLDEN DELIGHTS

¶ serves four
¶ 30–40 minutes

This orange steamed pudding is a filling dessert after a light meal. Serve it with Cup of Custard if you like.

1 cup whole wheat flour
2 teaspoons baking powder
1½ teaspoons dried orange peel
handful of golden raisins *or* diced apricots
3 tablespoons oil *or* butter
⅓ cup honey
1 egg
an orange *or* 8 apricot halves
2 tablespoons honey *or* golden syrup *or* jam

At Home: Combine the dry ingredients and the raisins in a zip-locking plastic bag. Pour the honey and oil into a plastic bottle. To avoid possible spills, but the bottle in another zip-locking plastic bag. Carry the egg and the orange or apricot halves separately.

In Camp: Add 3 *tablespoons* of water to the oil or butter and honey. Add the dry ingredients with the egg and mix well. If you took an orange, slice it thinly. In an oiled medium-size pot, place thin slices of orange, with the skin on, or the apricot halves. Pour on the honey, golden syrup, or jam. Put the pudding batter on top of this and cover with a tight-fitting lid (tied on), or foil. Steam for 30–40 minutes, following the basic steaming directions on page 22. The pudding should be springy to the touch. Make sure the lid is tied on or steam will get into the pudding bowl and make the pudding soggy.

STEAMED CHOCOLATE FUDGE PUDDING

¶ serves two
¶ 30–40 minutes

Chocolate decadence!

½ cup whole wheat flour
1 teaspoon baking powder
2 tablespoons cocoa
2 tablespoons chopped nuts (optional)
⅓ cup butter
¼ cup honey
1 teaspoon vanilla
1 egg

Topping:
½ cup honey
2 tablespoons cocoa

At Home: Combine the baking powder, cocoa, and nuts together in a zip-locking plastic bag. Combine the butter, honey, and vanilla in a plastic bottle. Carry the egg separately. Make sure you have the correct pot, at least 6 inches in diameter with a tightly fitting lid, or else carry foil to cover it. Combine the topping ingredients in another plastic bottle. To avoid possible spills, carry the bottles together in a zip-locking plastic bag.

In Camp: Combine the flour mixture, the butter mixture, the egg and *1 tablespoon* of water. Mix well. Place the batter in a medium-size oiled pot. Combine *¾ cup* of hot water with the topping mixture. Pour on top of batter. Place the lid on or make a lid of foil. Steam for 30–40 minutes, following the basic steaming instructions on page 22. Enjoy the pudding while it's warm.

GINGERBREAD

¶ serves two with leftovers for lunch
¶ 1 hour

This is a delicious, moist steamed bread. It does take 60 minutes to steam, but it is well worth the wait. It's a good recipe for a weekend trip with a special touch. If you just can't wait or your fuel is low, steam for 30 minutes for a "ginger goo pudding." Serve the gingerbread cold the next day with a sharp cheddar cheese. An epicurean delight!

1½ cups whole wheat flour *or* unbleached white
    flour
2 tablespoons buttermilk powder
1 tablespoon ginger
1 teaspoon cinnamon
1 teaspoon baking soda
½ cup unsulphured molasses
¼ cup honey (optional)
¼ cup butter
1 egg (optional)

At Home: Combine the dry ingredients in a zip-locking plastic bag. Combine the molasses, honey, and butter in a plastic bottle. For safety against spills, carry the bottle in another zip-locking plastic bag.

In Camp: Combine the two mixtures and mix in ⅓–½ *cup* of water. Stir well. Pour into a lightly greased medium-size cookpot. Refer to page 22 for steaming directions. The gingerbread will take a full hour to steam. It should be springy to the touch. If not, cover again and steam for 10 minutes more.

PINEAPPLE UPSIDE-DOWN CAKE

¶ serves two to four
¶ 20–25 minutes

For a backcountry birthday. Remember the candles!

½ cup whole wheat flour
⅓ cup brown rice flour
¼ cup milk powder
¼ cup raw wheat germ
1 teaspoon baking powder
¼ cup honey
2 tablespoons oil
1 teaspoon vanilla
4–6 dried pineapple rings

Topping:
½ cup walnuts or pecans
2 tablespoons butter
¼ cup honey

At Home: Combine the first five ingredients together in a zip-locking plastic bag. Combine the honey, oil, and vanilla in a plastic bottle. For safety against spills, put the bottle in another zip-locking plastic bag. Carry the pineapple separately. In a lidded container, combine the butter, honey, and nuts for the topping.

In Camp: Add the oil mixture to the dry ingredients with ⅓ cup of water. Mix well. In an oiled 7–8-inch pan, place the pineapple rings, whole or broken into small pieces. Pour the topping mixture over the pineapple, then top with the batter. Cover tightly, and bake at low heat. Use a heat diffuser between the pan and the stove if necessary. Cook for 20–25 minutes, or until the cake is springy to the touch.

SPICE CAKE

¶ serves two to four
¶ 30 minutes

Honey and spice and everything nice.

¾ cup whole wheat flour
¼ cup brown rice flour
¼ cup raw wheat germ
¼ cup milk powder
1 teaspoon baking powder
1 teaspoon cinnamon
½ teaspoon allspice
¼ teaspoon nutmeg
pinch cloves
pinch salt
small handful each, chopped walnuts, raisins,
    chopped dried apples
⅓ cup honey
¼ cup oil
1 teaspoon vanilla

At Home: Combine the dry ingredients in a zip-locking plastic bag. Combine the honey, oil, and vanilla in a plastic bottle. To avoid spills, put the bottle in another zip-locking plastic bag.

In Camp: Combine the two mixtures, and add ⅓ *cup* of water. Mix well. The batter should be slightly dry for quicker cooking. Spread in a 7-inch oiled pan.

COOKING METHOD 1: Cover the pan tightly with a lid or tie on a foil lid with string, and steam for 30–35 minutes, following steaming instructions on page 22.

COOKING METHOD 2: Cover the pan tightly with a lid or foil, and bake over moderate heat. Use a heat diffuser between the pan and the stove if necessary. Cook for 30 minutes, or until the cake is springy to the touch.

TOPPINGS

¶ enough for one 6-inch-pan cake

Basic Vanilla Topping:
2 tablespoons honey
1–1½ tablespoons butter
½ teaspoon vanilla

Carob Topping:
(add to Basic Vanilla Topping)
3 tablespoons carob powder

Crunchy Topping:
(add to Basic Vanilla Topping)
1 teaspoon date sugar

Spice Topping:
(add to Basic Vanilla Topping)
1 teaspoon date sugar (optional)
⅛ teaspoon cinnamon
dash cloves, nutmeg

DATE WALNUT TOPPING

¶ approximately ¾ cup

Serve this as a sweet topping on Meal Cakes, bread, or pancakes—hot or cold.

½ cup dates, pitted and sliced
¼ cup walnuts, chopped fine
½ cup water

In Camp: Place the ingredients in a cookpot. On low heat, stir until they are warmed through.

CITRUS CREAM CHEESE SPREAD

¶ 3 ounces

3 ounces cream cheese
rind of lemon *or* orange
1–2 tablespoons honey

At Home: Combine the ingredients in a zip-locking
plastic bag.

In Camp: Spread on cakes, crackers, breads, or
pancakes.

SNOW ICE CREAM

This is a delicious refresher—especially suited for
ski-touring trips and sweet moments.

Fill a cup with fresh, clean snow. Pour over
the snow:
apple or orange juice concentrate (may be bought
    in small cans) *or*
any berry concentrate (in small bottles) *or*
maple syrup *or*
Honey Syrup

Eat or drink.

BEVERAGES

It is important to get plenty of liquids while on the trail, as the extra energy you're using, the climate, and the altitude change can cause dehydration.

Mountain streams offer the best drink available—however, please read the precautions about water on page 11.

HERBAL TONIC TEAS

Tonics are herbs that have a generally invigorating and stimulating effect on the system, toning muscles and organs. Try some of these tonic teas and become familiar with the tastes and effects that suit you and your family and friends. We encourage you to take the time to discover and learn about some of these beneficial plants.

Here is a general list of tonic teas that may be easily purchased dried at natural food stores:

catnip leaves
celery seeds
chamomile flower tips
comfrey leaves
ginseng root
golden seal root
juniper berries
mugwort, whole plant
nettle flowers, leaves,
    and seeds
orange and lemon rinds

parsley leaves and root
peppermint leaves
raspberry leaves
red clover flower tips
rose hips
sage leaves
sassafras bark
thyme leaves
yarrow, whole plant
yellow dock root
yerba santa leaves

The standard amount of herbs to use is *1 teaspoon* per cup of water. In general, if you are using leaves and delicate parts, merely pour boiling water over them, steep for 5–10 minutes, strain, and serve. If you are using roots or bark, add them to the pot of boiling water, lower the heat, and boil from 15–30 minutes.

Combinations of teas are a good idea, and you will soon find combinations that suit your needs and taste. Usually we combine two or three, but certainly more may be used.

Also, it is a good idea to switch herbs from time to time, so your system doesn't get saturated with any particular one. Dried tea leaves are very lightweight and the most rewarding drink we can recommend aside from pure water. Honey may be added to any of these tonic teas.

SUN-INFUSED HERBAL TEA

¶ 1 quart

Early in the morning, as soon as you feel the sun beginning to warm your body, collect *4 cups of fresh or purified water* in a plastic quart bottle with a lid. Add *4 teaspoons dried herbs* and set the bottle in the sun on a rock. Let it sit until the sun starts to go down, then strain and serve. You might want to put the bottle in a creek to cool it before straining.

SUN-INFUSED HERBAL LEMONADE

¶ 1 quart

This is a luxury for the little ones who might be accompanying you on your journey. Follow directions for Sun-Infused Herbal Tea, except add *4 tablespoons of lemon juice* and *2 tablespoons of honey* when you add the herbs. Especially good for children are peppermint, chamomile, catnip, alfalfa, hyssop, and comfrey. These may be used individually or in combinations of two or three. This is a sunshine-sweet drink!

ROSE HIP DRINK

¶ 3 cups

This is very good on a cold winter night or early in the morning when your tent is still frost-covered; it's high in vitamin C.

2 tablespoons rose hip powder
¼ cup maple syrup (also available powdered)
3 cups water

Combine, heat, and serve

LEMONADE

¶ 1 cup

Lemons are the best thirst quenchers. Take a few lemons for lemonade. One lemon in a gallon of water will keep the water fresh if you have to carry it for several days.

2 tablespoons lemon juice
2 teaspoons honey
1 cup water

Combine. You may have to use ¼ *cup* hot water first to dissolve the honey and then add ¾ *cup* cold. For hot days, prepare the lemonade in the morning, put in a lidded plastic bottle, and place securely in a stream. In cold weather, however, this is very good heated.

LEMON WATER

This is very refreshing, and it feels good in your mouth. Try this recipe using lime, too.

Squeeze *half a lemon* in your cup, and fill the cup with cold water. Swish it around and drink. This is better than powdered mixes.

FRUIT JUICE CONCENTRATES

Most natural food stores have this product available without added sugar (the proportion of concentrate to water is usually 1 to 5, but some vary—it will say on the bottle). Fruit juice concentrates are a real treat, on winter expeditions they add a touch of fresh fruit flavor. To mention a few: red and black raspberry, blueberry, black currant, apricot, blackberry, peach, plum, grape, black cherry, cranberry, boysenberry.

We recommend rationing these drinks carefully, as the liquid concentrates add up fast, weight-wise, and money-wise, but they are refreshing, sweet-tasting liquid, besides being a very good tonic drink, and we suggest you try a little bit for at least one hot afternoon. These drinks are also very good warm, for cold mornings and evenings. Children will love you for taking the trouble to pack them.

HORCHATA

¶ 1 quart

This is a nutritious Latin American drink. Serve it iced or hot.

1½ cups pumpkin seeds, ground
1 cup brown rice flour
⅔ cup almonds, ground
4 tablespoons cinnamon, roasted
1½ cups milk powder

At Home: Grind seeds and nuts in a nut or coffee grinder. Roast the cinnamon over moderate heat in a dry frying pan, stirring constantly, until the aroma changes. Cool. Combine all the ingredients in a zip-locking plastic bag.

In Camp:

COLD: Place *1 cup* of the Horchata mixture in a container, and slowly stir in *1 quart* of cold water. Let the mixture stand 1 hour, covered. Shake or mix well and serve. Strain if desired. Sweeten with honey or maple syrup.

HOT: Place *1 cup* of the Horchata mixture in your cookpot, and slowly stir in *1 quart* of water. Bring to a boil over moderate heat, stirring constantly. Cook about 1 minute, or until the mixture thickens. Strain, if desired, and serve. Sweeten with honey or maple syrup.

Variations: Add ½ cup cocoa to the dry mixture, roasting the cocoa with the cinnamon; add 1 teaspoon freshly ground allspice to the dry mixture.

ANISE MILK DRINK

¶ 1 quart

The delicate flavor of anise makes this sweet drink a favorite.

1¼ cups milk powder
1 teaspoon anise seeds
2 tablespoons honey
butter, for hot drink

COLD: Make this on a day when you are going on a day hike away from camp and know you will want a good drink when you return. In a plastic quart bottle, combine the milk powder, honey, and anise in 2–3 *cups* of water. Put on the lid and shake well. Set the bottle on a rock where the sun will hit it all day. When you return to camp in the evening, fill the rest of the bottle full of water and shake. If it is still too warm, place the bottle carefully in a stream for a short while if possible. Strain and serve.

HOT: Combine all the ingredients with 4 *cups* of water in your cookpot. Stir well and heat through until quite warm, but do not boil. Remove from heat, cover, and let sit for 5 minutes. Strain into cups and add a lump of butter in each cup. Children love it!

CAROB MILK

This milk drink is a healthy replacement for chocolate milk. It's high in calcium and food energy and builds the body rather than tearing it down.

1 cup milk powder
⅓ cup carob powder
1 tablespoon honey (optional)
½ teaspoon vanilla

COLD: Put 3 *cups* of cold water in a plastic quart bottle. Add the milk powder and carob. Screw the lid on tight and shake well to mix. Stir the honey in a small container or cup with a little bit of warm water to dissolve it. Add the honey and vanilla to the quart bottle, and fill it almost to the top with cold water. Shake again, and serve.

HOT: Combine all ingredients with 4 *cups* of water in a cookpot. Heat, stirring frequently; do not boil. Serve when hot.

Variation: Add 1 teaspoon of dry malt powder.

CASHEW MILK

¶ 2 cups

This is also delicious poured over hot cereal or pudding, millet and dates, rice and raisins. It's also a refreshing drink for small children.

1 cup raw cashews, ground fine
1 tablespoon honey
1 teaspoon vanilla

At Home: Grind the nuts in a blender, coffee grinder, or food mill, and mix in the vanilla and honey. Carry in a plastic bottle.

In Camp or On the Trail: Slowly add *2 cups* water and mix well.

Variation: For almond milk, follow the recipe but blanch and peel the almonds first.

CONDIMENTS

Stewed Fruit, Raisin Sauce,
Cheese Toasties, Sesame Salt, Wakame,
and other miscellaneous recipes.

STEWED FRUIT

¶ approximately 2–3 cups

This is a light breakfast by itself. It can be made heartier served with Drop Scones and peanut butter. Or add some spices and serve for dessert, hot or cold.

Soak 2 cups of any combination of unsulphured dried fruit overnight with water to cover 1 inch above the fruit. In the morning, simmer, covered, over low heat for 5–10 minutes. Use a heat diffuser if necessary to prevent sticking.

Stewed Fruit is good over granola, pancakes, cornbread, grains, hot cereal, and Meal Cakes.

Variations: Add lemon, orange, cinnamon, and/or cloves.

For Dried Fruit Jam: Barely cover the fruit with water and soak for 10 minutes. Add *1 tablespoon of honey* per cup of fruit. Simmer until thick, stirring occasionally. Try apricots and dates together.

For Stewed Fruit Soup with Dumplings: Use more water to make a broth. Bring to a boil. Plop Whole Wheat Spice Dumplings into the bubbling fruit and then follow instructions on page 136.

RAISIN SAUCE FOR PANCAKES

¶ 2¼ cups
¶ 3 minutes

¾ cup mixed golden raisins, currants, raisins,
    and dates
1 tablespoon cornstarch
honey to taste
1 teaspoon cinnamon
¼ teaspoon nutmeg
pinch ground cloves

At Home: Combine all the ingredients in a zip-locking plastic bag.

In Camp: Place the ingredients in a cookpot, and slowly add *1½ cups* of water. Cook over moderate heat, stirring until the mixture boils and thickens. Serve the sauce over pancakes or puddings.

Variations: Add citrus rinds or any dried fruit; use maple sugar instead of honey; omit the listed spices and add 1 tablespoon of ground ginger.

CHEESE TOASTIES

Take pieces of bread, Journey Cakes, crackers, pancakes, or leftover patties, and put slices of cheese on them. (Butter the bread first if desired.) Place in a pan, cover, and heat over a low flame. Toast until the cheese melts. Serve with soup or stew.

GARLIC BREAD

Melt some butter in a cookpot, and add a few sliced garlic cloves. Then start toasting bread slices in a pan over low heat. When one side is done, turn it, spoon on the garlic butter, and continue toasting. You can use garlic granules instead of fresh garlic.

POPPED SEEDS

Heat a pan over moderate heat and add 1 cup, mixed or by themselves: hulled pumpkin seeds, sunflower seeds, squash seeds. Toast lightly stirring constantly. When all seem to have popped or become brown, add 1–2 teaspoons of soy sauce per cup of seeds and stir well and quickly, as the sauce crystallizes rapidly. Put in bowl or plate and let cool a bit before eating.

WAKAME

■■■

¶ serves two
¶ 10–15 minutes

This is a seaweed condiment for rice or other grains.

¼ cup dried wakame, cut in ½-inch lengths
2 tablespoons onion flakes
½ cup water
1 teaspoon oil

Soak the wakame and onion in the water for 15 minutes. Strain and reserve the liquid. Put the oil in a frying pan, add the seaweed and onions, and stir-fry for a few minutes. Add the reserved liquid and bring to a boil. Reduce the heat and cook 5–10 minutes.

Garnishes: ¾ teaspoon lemon juice; ¾ teaspoon tamari soy sauce; stir in ¾ teaspoon miso paste.

TOASTED NORI

■■■

These paper-thin sheets of seaweed may be lightly toasted over an open flame. Simply run them quickly through the flame until their color changes and they get crispy. Break them in small pieces as a garnish for soups and grains or eat them plain. They're very nourishing.

Variation: Rub with sesame oil before toasting.

BASIL SALT

This is an aromatic salt to sprinkle. Don't be
limited to basil—try any herb or combination. To
1 part of herbs, add 2 *parts of sea salt.* Grind them
together in a coffee grinder, blender, or with mortar and pestle, or roll them with a rolling pin to
crush. Carry in a shaker bottle.

SESAME SALT

¶ approximately 1 cup

Known as *gomasio* to some, this wonderful garnish
not only heightens flavor, but also adds the valu-
able food energy of the sesame seed. In a short
time you will find yourself sprinkling it on everything you ever used just plain salt on.

1¼ cups sesame seeds, unhulled
1 tablespoon sea salt (or to taste)

Roast the sesame seeds in an unoiled frying pan
over moderate heat, stirring constantly until the
seeds darken and begin to pop (about 5 minutes).
Then combine the seeds with the salt. Grind with
mortar and pestle, coffee grinder, or a blender.
Store in an airtight container.

HOME-DRIED MUSHROOMS

Wash 1 or more pounds of mushrooms and gently wipe them dry. String with a needle and heavy thread, with the needle going through the center of the mushroom from top to bottom. Hang horizontally until dry, about 3 days.

HONEY SYRUP

¶ approximately 1 cup

This syrup can be made at home or in camp. It's very simple to make, and warmed up before serving it really makes pancakes seem luxurious.

1 cup honey
1 tablespoon water
1 teaspoon vanilla

Warm the honey, add the water and vanilla, and stir well. Heat over low heat until the honey is syrupy. If you make it at home, put it in a squeeze bottle and carry it ready to pour. Reheat it in camp, if you like, by submerging the bottle in hot water while the pancakes cook.

NATURAL REMEDIES

This section provides a general introduction to natural health aids. It is not meant to replace any standard first aid or medical manual (see page 246 for two good ones), but to add to it. Many minor ailments and discomforts that occur every now and then can be easily soothed by things you might be carrying in your pack: herbs, natural oils, vitamins, honey, garlic, lemons, dried fruit.

If any infection or ailment gets out of hand, or looks like it might, get to a lower elevation as soon as possible—as most problems will decrease at lower altitudes. Some problems may even disappear. If not, contact a physician. Remember, too, not to get too cold, tired, sweaty, or overextended on a hike.

Take it easy, climb slowly. The air is thinner at higher altitudes, making it easier to get sunburned. Drink a lot of water and use more salt to prevent dehydration.

Take care.

TEAS AND POULTICES

Finding yourself along the trail or arriving in camp with an unexpected ache or pain can be very unpleasant unless you stay on top of the situation and use a little common sense. Usually water, soap, salt, honey, and the right foods will take care of minor complaints. We list below a few herb teas. The wonderful benefit of these teas is that they may be taken at any time, as they have a "toning" effect on the body. So if you invest in a small amount of herbs to take along for specific reasons, and no one gets hurt or sick, you will still have many delicious cups of tea at hand that your body will appreciate. Herbs keep very well—for at least a year, and some of them several years, if packaged airtight—and are lightweight to pack in. For general information about herb teas, see Herbal Tonic Teas on pages 213.

cayenne, powdered
chamomile blossoms
chickweed leaves
comfrey, root and
    leaves
flaxseed
ginger, powdered
ginseng, powdered
golden seal, powdered

juniper berries
parsley leaves
pennyroyal leaves
peppermint leaves
plantain leaves
sage leaves
scullcap leaves and
    stems
squaw tea (stems)

How to Make a Poultice: To make a poultice, use either fresh or dried and ground herbs. Wash the affected area and apply either fresh herbs that have been bruised or crushed in some way (either between your hands, with a rock, or by chewing them a little) and thereby moistened in their own juices, or dried herbs you have brought along. If the dried herbs are not powdery, try to get them as much so as possible by crushing with your fingertips, rubbing between flat rocks, or pulverizing them in a cup with a wooden spoon. Add enough water to make a paste that is not runny, mixing well. Cover the poultice with a dressing of a plastic nature (see Bleeding, below) to hold the moisture of the herb directly on the affected area for several hours.

Altitude Sickness: See Stress and Inability to Adjust to Altitude Change, page 235.

Bleeding: From *minor* cuts or wounds. Wash the wound well with water to which you have added a few drops of liquid soap, or with a mild normal salt solution: *1 level teaspoon* of salt to *1 cup* (8 ounces) water. (If you add too much salt, it will sting.) You may sprinkle on powdered cayenne to stop the bleeding. A cool poultice of comfrey or plantain may be applied. Cover the afflicted area with a sterile, or as clean as possible, cloth or a dressing and apply light pressure. Make a tea of comfrey, plantain, or cayenne, and drink it right away. If the bleeding is excessive or if there are any signs of complications, be sure to get to a doctor right away.

Blisters: Don't open. If the blister should break open, immediately wash well with soap and water, let dry, and apply wheat germ oil or vitamin E cream, or even olive oil, if that's all you have. Cover with a Band-Aid until healed, applying fresh oil and changing the bandage as needed. Plantain, comfrey, or golden seal may be used also as a poultice. For blistered feet, we recommend moleskins. Dr. Scholl's Moleskin can be found in any drugstore. Cut a hole about ½ inch bigger than the blister in the center of a square of moleskin. Press on your foot, cover with a sock, and keep the area clean. After the blister opens, apply an oil, as mentioned above, if possible.

Bruises: For bad bruises, make a warm poultice of comfrey, pennyroyal or cayenne and while it is still warm, put it directly on the bruise. Cover the poultice and let it sit on the bruise for 5 minutes or so. Remove, apply a fresh poultice, and cover with a dressing. Leave both on overnight. Repeat if necessary. You may gently rub on wheat germ oil from time to time.

Burns (Minor): A burn is an open wound, and it should be treated as such. Immediately immerse the area in cold water for 5 minutes or so. Remove from the water, and, in order to clean any possible dirt out, pour soap and water or a saltwater solution (*1 teaspoon* salt to *1 cup* of cold water) over the burn. (Avoid bothering the area as much as possible.) Carefully pat dry and air briefly. A cool or body-temperature healing poultice of powdered golden seal, comfrey, or plantain may be applied, or cover the area with honey or olive or wheat germ oil. Apply a clean fluffy dressing or cloth. Keep covered for 3 days before changing the dressing, if possible.

Chapped Skin, Sunburn, Windburn: Rub in wheat germ, olive, apricot, or almond oil. In the case of sunburn, swim in cold water or apply a cold wet cloth. Stay in the shade. Reapply oils as often as your body soaks them in.

Cold: Wear wool shirts and sweaters, as wool keeps you warm even when it's wet. We recommend layering—using cotton under wool clothing. To prevent getting chilled, the minute you start perspiring take off the top layer until you're down to your skin, if you have to be. As soon as you stop working hard, start putting the layers back on, slowly, to retain the body heat that you've built up from working and sweating. If you get chilled before you put your clothes back on, it's very hard to get warm again. We have found that carrying the little extra weight of wool clothing will pay off. Keep a hat on—you lose a lot of heat through the top of your head.

Winter Tea to Warm You Up: A stimulating, energizing tea is a combination of ginseng, cayenne, ginger, and juniper berries. Serve with lemon juice and drink hot.

Cuts and Scrapes: Wash well, soak in saltwater (*1 level teaspoon* of salt per *cup* of water). Keep clean and free of infection. Apply wheat germ oil or vitamin E cream or oil. A tea or poultice may be made of comfrey, plantain, golden seal, or chamomile. Either bathe the area with tea or cover with a body-temperature poultice. Keep soft with oil. Cover with a Band-Aid. Change as necessary.

Eye Burn from Glare, Snow, and/or Sun: Make a tea of chamomile or chickweed. Soak a cloth in the tea when it's cool. Put the wet cloth over your closed eyes, being sure that a few drops get into them to rinse them somewhat. Repeat three times for 5 minutes each time.

Fatigue: Fatigue is often caused by heat intoxication (a major loss of fluids and salt, causing a state of dizziness, lightheadedness, and even shock. It is not to be confused with *heat stroke*, in which the afflicted person gets red in the face, has a very high fever, and loses as much as a quarter of body weight). For fatigue, take extra salt, drink *lots* of water to which honey has been added, if possible. Try to sleep or just rest. Make sure you can breathe freely. Don't overeat, keep bowels loose, and drink hot tea of ginseng, cayenne, or peppermint. (See also: Hypothermia.)

Food Shortage: If your food supply becomes dangerously low, and you need every bit of nutrition you can find, drink comfrey, sage, or squaw tea, or make a weak solution (*1 tablespoon per cup*) of rice, rye, or oats, and drink it as a tea. These are very lightweight, so pack in a bit extra for emergencies.

Headache: Drink lots of water. Note whether the problem stems from heat, fatigue, nerves, or eye strain, and if so, follow those particular remedies. Headaches are also often caused by constipation.

If you are sure that this is the case, drink lots of water; eat purgative fruits and drink their juices; drink 4–5 cups a day of tea made of chickweed, ginger, peppermint, and/or cayenne. If the problem persists, or is serious, or might be a sign of another problem, be sure to see a doctor.

Heat: Drink a lot of liquids, and use extra salt. Wear cotton clothing, as its natural fibers breathe better than those of nylon and other synthetics. Wear a light-colored straw or cotton hat. For an exhilarating treat, dip the top of your head in a stream and let the cool water run down your face when you stand up. Sometimes it feels good and helps to soak a bandana handkerchief in a stream and wrap it loosely around your neck. Try washing your hands and arms to the elbows with water; even soaking your feet for a few minutes will help. Ben Kinmont likes to soak his hat in a creek, fill it with water, and dump the water on top of his head as he puts his hat on.

Summer Tea to Cool You Down: This tea could be started early in the morning, put in the sun, and then left securely in a creek just before lunch or in the early afternoon. In the heat of the day when you are tired of frolicking, sit in the shade and drink it. Or the tea could be made in the morning and carried along on hikes until it is cooler and the sun is hotter. Use chickweed, plantain, and/or peppermint. Serve with lemon juice, if you have some. Drink lots.

Hypothermia: This is as acute as heat stroke, only in the opposite direction. Hypothermia means basically that a person is cold clear to the bone, and that all of the body's defensive resources are nearly exhausted. If the person gets any colder, she or he will die. When in this state, a person no longer has the ability to realize that he or she is cold. It could happen under any particular set of circumstances—after a rainstorm or a fall in a lake, or whatever, and it is a critical condition that should be treated at once. The individual should be warmed immediately—wrapped in a sleeping bag (preferably with another person for that person's body heat), put by a warm fire, and given warm, nutritional teas with honey.

Infections, Skin (minor): Make a poultice of dried ground plantain or comfrey and warm water, cover the infection, and put on a Band-Aid. If no herbs are available, make a compress with warm salt-water (*1 level teaspoon* of salt per *cup* of water) and apply. Change the poultice every couple of hours or so. If you are using saltwater, soak the area 4–6 times a day, trying to bring the infection to a head. If possible, drink tea of golden seal powder (*1 cup* 3 times a day) or take it in capsules (1 capsule 3 times a day). When the infection comes to a head, sterilize a knife (everyone should have a good sharp knife along) with a flame or by boiling or with soap and water; make a cut where the head is large enough that you don't have to squeeze hard (if you apply too much pressure, you'll break down the wall around the infection, and it might travel elsewhere); remove the pus by flushing the wound with cold fresh water, and treat the infection as a cut or scrape.

Lack of Fresh Food: Take extra vitamin C (try to get organic vitamin C) or take vitamin B complex, or a tea of either or both juniper berries and flax-seed. Keep handy, especially on winter trips.

Mosquito Bites: Warm, sweaty skin attracts mosquitos. Rub on pennyroyal or eucalyptus oil, and take vitamin B complex daily. Put lemon juice or vinegar on bites. Mosquito repellent: 1 part citronella, 1 part spirit of camphor, ½ part oil of cedar; mix with a little olive oil. For sensitive skin, add more oil.

Muscle Pain: Remember that a charley horse is a muscle spasm. Treat muscle aches by stretching and using the muscles, as the pain is caused by muscle contraction. If you stop using them altogether, your muscles will tighten and get sorer. If possible, apply warm compresses of cloth soaked in chamomile or comfrey tea. Resoak the cloth every 15 minutes or so and repeat for 1 hour.

Nerves, Calmatives: It's hard to imagine anyone needing one of these teas in the backcountry, but you never know. Take a cup of warm tea three times a day or before going to bed of any one or combination of the following: chamomile, scullcap, golden seal, or peppermint. Chew on fresh pennyroyal leaves, if available.

Stress and Inability to Adjust to Altitude Change: Symptoms: A combination of headache, fever, extreme fatigue, quick shallow breathing, sweating, and nausea. First thing to do is to lie down and rest. If the problem isn't solved by resting, go to a lower elevation. Drink lots of water and take diuretic teas—any of the following: plantain, parsley, juniper berries, chamomile, scullcap, golden seal, flaxseed, or buchu leaves.

APPENDICES

MENUS

Here are four menu plans: one for an extensive 10-day trip, one for the usual weekend or 3-day trip, a cookless menu, and one for special occasions and celebrations.

The 10-day menu is planned with higher-protein meals toward the end when you will need the protein the most. The 3-day menu includes more fresh foods and weight per day, since it's easier to carry relatively heavier loads per day on short trips.

Cookless meals in the backcountry are easy and convenient. However, we recommend carrying a stove to make hot tea or soup in case the weather turns cold.

Cook extra pancakes for breakfast and save the leftovers for lunch. Plan some drinks ahead of time so they will be ready when you return from a hike.

The foods used here are all long-lasting, with the exception of the fresh fruits, vegetables, and cheeses. The fresh foods will usually last up to a week. To preserve cheese a while longer for extensive trips or for food caches, wrap it in cheesecloth, dip it in melted wax, and let it set. Butter will last for a couple of weeks if carried in a plastic container and stored in the shade.

10-DAY MENU FOR TWO

BREAKFAST SUGGESTIONS

Hot Cracked Millet Cream Cereal with milk

Corn Pancakes with peanut butter and
    maple syrup

Boston Brown Bread with cream cheese
Hot Carob Drink

Oatmeal Pancakes with honey and butter

Stewed Fruit over Granola
Mint Tea

Wheat Germ Cereal with prunes
Hot Carob Drink

Whole Wheat Soy Pancakes with Raisin Sauce

Drop Scones with herbs and Tahini Orange Sauce
    or Cashew Gravy

Stewed Fruit with Cornbread

Mountain Gruel Cereal
Tea

LUNCH SUGGESTIONS

High-Protein Crackers and cheese
Polenta Cakes with Cream of Celery Soup
Soybean Burgers with cheese
Leftover pancakes or bread with nut butters
Miso Sesame Butter Spread on Lentil Rice Cakes
Five-Grain Soup with Carrot Cakes
Cheese
Dried fruit
Nuts
Popped Seeds or Toasted Soybeans
Peanut Butter Fudge, 1 pound
Seed Date Fudge, ½ pound
Oranges
Anzacs

Fruit Leather
Lemons for Lemonade
And all the good leftovers

Spinach Cheese Soup
Sesame Seed Crackers
Fresh fruit

Spicy Hot and Sour Soup
Apple Crisp
Hot Chocolate

Minted Cream of Pea Soup
Whole Wheat Bread and butter

Seafood Curry over Basmati Rice
Whole Wheat Irish Soda Bread with raisins

Miso Soup
Fruit and Noodle Salad
Anzacs

Salsa Soup with Corn Cheese Dumplings
Creamy Tapioca Pudding

One-Pot Grain and Seafood
Pineapple Upside-Down Cake

Cream of Tomato Soup
Dilly Dumplings
Cornbread

Spiced Tomato Millet Soup
Crackers
Golden Delights

Minestrone Soup and Cheese Cookies

3-DAY MENU FOR TWO

Breakfast Suggestions

Hot Cracked Millet Cream with Cashew Milk

Moroccan Couscous with eggs and Carrot Cakes

Buckwheat Pancakes with Raisin Sauce

Lunch Suggestions

Potato Cakes with hot mustard
Boiled Fruit Cake

Cheese, dried fruit and nuts, Lemonade, Coconut
    Almond Barley Cakes

Crackers with Humus, fresh vegetables

All the good leftovers

Dinner Suggestions

Falafel and cucumbers in pocket bread with Tahini
    Dipping Sauce
Truly Fruity Bars

Salmon in Tomato Orange Sauce over rice or pasta
Spice Cake

Spicy Hot and Sour Soup
Oriental Brown Rice Cakes
Gingerbread

COOKLESS MENU

BREAKFAST SUGGESTIONS:

Granola or
Soaked Cereal

LUNCH SUGGESTIONS:

Pumpkin Pie Cakes or Boston Brown Bread with
　　Cheese Spread

DINNER SUGGESTIONS:

Polenta Cakes
Peanut butter
Cheese
Fruitcake

MENU FOR CELEBRATIONS

Fondue with French bread and vegetable sticks
for dipping
Pineapple Upside-Down Cake
Wine

Crab a la King over rice or pasta
Steamed Chocolate Fudge Pudding

Shrimp Curry over brown rice
Whole Wheat Bread
Apricot Date Fudge

Fruit and Noodle Salad
Gingerbread with whipped cream
Horchata

FOOD SOURCES

Any natural food store, grocery, or supermarket.

International food stores: Japanese, Chinese, East Indian, Asian, Latin American, and so on.

Bulk Dehydrated and Freeze-Dried Foods

Ken's Mountaineering and Backpacking
155 North Edison Way
Reno, NV 89502

Quinoa:

The Quinoa Corporation
P.O. Box 7114
Boulder, CO 80306
(303) 444–9462

Instant Wild Rice:

Gibbs Wild Rice Company, Inc.
Rt. 2
Deer River, MN 56636
(218) 246–8505

Water Filter:

General Ecology Inc.
151 Sherree Road
Lionville, PA 19353

BOOKS TO READ
AND USE

ABBEY, Edward. Any of his writings.

BOONE, J. Allen. *Kinship with All Life*. New York:
Harper & Row, 1954.

BROWN, Edward Espe. *Tassajara Cooking*.
Berkeley: Shambala, 1973.

DARVILL, Fred T., Jr., M.D. *Medicine for
Mountaineering*. Seattle: The
Mountaineers, 1967.

DOYLE, Helen Macknight. *Doctor Nellie:
Autobiography of Helen Macknight Doyle*.
Edited and published by Ginny Smith.
Mammoth Lakes, Calif.: Ginny Smith, 1983.
(Distributed by William Kaufmann,
Los Altos, Calif.)

HART, John. *Walking Softly in the Wilderness,
Sierra Club Guide to Backpacking*.
San Francisco: Sierra Club Books,
revised edition, 1984.

KLOSS, Jethro. *Back to Eden*. Coalmont, Tenn.:
Longview Publishing House, 1970.

LAPPÈ, Frances Moore. *Diet for a Small Planet*.
10th anniversary ed. New York: Friends of the
Earth/Ballantine Books, 1982.

STEWART, Elinore Pruitt. *Letters of a Woman
Homesteader*. Lincoln: University of Nebraska
Press/Bison Books, 1967.

STORM, Hyemeyohsts. *Seven Arrows*. New York:
Harper & Row, 1972.

MUIR, John. *The Wilderness World of John Muir*.
Edited by Edwin Way Teal. Boston: Houghton
Mifflin, 1954. Or any of Muir's works.

TOMPKINS, Peter, and Christopher Bird.
The Secret Life of Plants. New York:
Avon Books, 1973.

WILKERSON, James A., *Medicine for
Mountaineering*. Seattle: The
Mountaineers, 1967.

With all that evolving spread out behind us
We dance this frost fall morning away
On the sunward sides
Of granite boulders

Doug Robinson

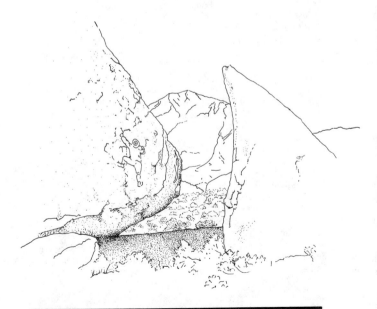

INDEX
